W9-AYK-202

Born After Midnight

by A. W. TOZER

§

CHRISTIAN PUBLICATIONS, INC.

HARRISBURG, PENNSYLVANIA

Christian Publications, Inc.
25 S. 10th Street, P.O. Box 3404
Harrisburg, PA 17105

The mark of ℗ *vibrant faith*

ISBN 0-87509-167-9
Printed in the United States of America

Foreword

To SPEAK to God on behalf of men is probably the highest service any of us can render. The next is to speak to men in the name of God. Either is a privilege possible to us only through the grace of our Lord Jesus Christ.

To sit even for a moment in the chair of the teacher and write that which may affect the life and character of numerous persons is not only a lofty privilege but a grave responsibility as well.

The only qualifications I bring to the writing of these pages are love for the Triune Godhead and a sorrowful concern for the spiritual welfare of the Church which our Lord purchased with His own blood.

If there is anything here good or helpful to the children of God it must be attributed to the operation of the Holy Spirit who often condescends to work through unworthy instruments. Whatever else may be found here is due to human weakness and is better forgotten.

My prayers go with this book and with all who may chance to read it.

A. W. TOZER.

Chicago, Illinois
July 22, 1959

Contents

Chapter 1

Born After Midnight

AMONG REVIVAL-MINDED Christians I have heard the saying, "Revivals are born after midnight."

This is one of those proverbs which, while not quite literally true, yet points to something very true.

If we understand the saying to mean that God does not hear our prayer for revival made in the daytime, it is of course not true. If we take it to mean that prayer offered when we are tired and worn-out has greater power than prayer made when we are rested and fresh, again it is not true. God would need to be very austere indeed to require us to turn our prayer into penance, or to enjoy seeing us punish ourselves by intercession. Traces of such ascetical notions are still found among some gospel Christians, and while these brethren are to be commended for their zeal, they are not to be excused for unconsciously attributing to God a streak of sadism unworthy of fallen men.

Yet there is considerable truth in the idea that revivals are born after midnight, for revivals (or any other spiritual gifts and graces) come only to those who want them badly enough. It may be said without qualification that every man is as holy and as full of the Spirit as he wants to be. He may not be as full as he wishes he were, but he is most certainly as full as he wants to be.

Our Lord placed this beyond dispute when He said, "Blessed are they which do hunger and thirst after righteousness: for they shall be filled." Hunger and thirst are physical sensations which, in their acute stages, may become real pain. It has been the experience of countless seekers after God that when their desires became a pain they were suddenly and wonderfully filled. The problem is not to persuade God to fill us, but to want God sufficiently to permit Him to do so. The average Christian is so cold and so contented with His wretched condition that there is no vacuum of desire into which the blessed Spirit can rush in satisfying fullness.

Occasionally there will appear on the religious scene a man whose unsatisfied spiritual longings become so big and important in his life that they crowd out every other interest. Such a man refuses to be content with the safe and conventional prayers of the frost-bound brethren who "lead in prayer" week after week and year after year in the local assemblies. His yearnings carry him away and often make something of a nuisance out of him. His puzzled fellow Christians shake their heads and look knowingly at each other, but like the blind man who cried after his sight and was rebuked by the disciples, he "cries the more a great deal." And if he has not yet met the conditions or there is something hindering the answer to his prayer, he may pray on into the late hours. Not the hour of night but the state of his heart decides the time of his visitation. For him it may well be that revival comes after midnight.

It is very important, however, that we understand that long prayer vigils, or even strong crying and tears, are not in themselves meritorious acts. Every blessing flows out of the goodness of God as from a fountain. Even those rewards for good works about which certain teachers talk so fulsomely, and which they always set in sharp contrast to the benefits received by grace alone, are at bottom as certainly of grace as is the forgiveness of sin itself. The holiest apostle can claim no more than that he is an unprofitable servant. The very angels exist out of the pure goodness of God. No creature can "earn" anything in the usual meaning of the word. All things are by and of the sovereign goodness of God.

Lady Julian summed it up quaintly when she wrote, "It is more honor to God, and more very delight, that we faithfully pray to Himself of His goodness and cleave thereunto by His grace, and with true understanding, and steadfast by love, than if we took all the means that heart can think. For if we took all those means it is too little, and not full honor to God. But in His goodness is all the whole, and there faileth right nought . . . For the goodness of God is the highest prayer, and it cometh down to the lowest part of our need."

Yet for all God's good will toward us He is unable to grant us our heart's desires till all our desires have been reduced to one. When we have dealt with our carnal ambitions; when we have trodden upon the lion and adder of the flesh, have trampled the dragon of self-love under our feet and have truly reckoned ourselves to have died unto sin, then and only then can God raise us to newness of life and fill us with His blessed Holy Spirit.

It is easy to learn the doctrine of personal revival and victorious living; it is quite another thing to take our cross and plod on to the dark and bitter hill of self-renunciation. Here many are called and few are chosen. For every one that actually crosses over into the Promised Land there are many who stand for a while and look longingly across the river and then turn sadly back to the comparative safety of the sandy wastes of the old life.

No, there is no merit in late hour prayers, but it requires a serious mind and a determined heart to pray past the ordinary into the unusual. Most Christians never do. And it is more than possible that the rare soul who presses on into the unusual experience reaches there after midnight.

Chapter 2

The Missing Witness

ONE CAUSE OF the decline in the quality of religious experience among Christians these days is the neglect of the doctrine of the inward witness.

Stamping our feet to start the circulation and blowing on our hands to limber them up, we have emerged shivering from the long period of the theological deep-freeze, but the influence of the frosty years is still felt among us to such an extent that the words *witness, experience* and *feeling* are cautiously avoided by the rank and file of evangelical teachers. In spite of the undeniable lukewarmness of most of us we still fear that unless we keep a careful check on ourselves we shall surely lose our dignity and become howling fanatics by this time next week. We set a watch upon our emotions day and night lest we become over-spiritual and bring reproach upon the cause of Christ. Which all, if I may say so, is for most of us about as sensible as throwing a cordon of police around a cemetery to prevent a wild political demonstration by the inhabitants.

We who hold the doctrines of the New Testament these days believe ourselves to be in direct lineal descent from the apostles and true and legitimate offspring of the Early Church. Well, I believe there are today some who belong to the household of God, who are of the chosen generation and make up the royal priesthood and the holy nation of which Peter writes. They are found scattered among the churches where, we may as well admit, they are often a source of embarrassment to the mixed multitude that composes the membership. That much is true; but for us to assume that all evangelicals belong in the apostolic succession is to be too optimistic for our own good. So to believe suggests a disquieting parallel with those scribes and Pharisees of Jesus' day who claimed spiritual descent from Abraham because they could demonstrate that they were his physical offspring. "We be Abraham's seed," they boasted. Jesus replied by making a distinction. "I know that ye are Abraham's seed," He told them. "If ye were Abraham's children, ye would do the works of Abraham."

In the same way as the Pharisees we may err gravely by assuming that we are children of God because we hold the creed of God. It most certainly does not follow. It is not physical descent that marks one a true child of Abraham, for Abraham is the father of such as have faith, and faith is not passed on by natural procreation. So it is not creedal descent that proves us to be true sons of Pentecost, but identity of spirit with them upon whose heads sat the cloven tongues like as of fire.

One distinguishing mark of those first Christians was a supernatural radiance that shined out from within them. The sun had come up in their hearts and its warmth and light made unnecessary any secondary sources of assurance. They had the inner witness. They knew with an immediate awareness that required no jockeying of evidence to give them a feeling of certainty. Great power and great grace marked their lives, enabling them to rejoice to suffer shame for the name of Jesus.

It is obvious that the average evangelical Christian today is without this radiance. The efforts of some of our teachers to cheer up our drooping spirits are futile because those same teachers reject the very phenomenon that would naturally produce joy, namely, the inner witness. In their strange fear of the religious emotions they have explained away the Scriptures that teach this witness, such as, "The Spirit itself beareth witness" and "He that believeth on the Son of God hath the witness in himself."

Instead of the inner witness we now substitute logical conclusions drawn from texts. A conversation between a seeker and a worker in an inquiry room is likely to run about like this: "Do you want the Lord to receive you and make you His child?" "Yes." "Well, read this: 'Him that cometh to me I will in no wise cast out.' Do you believe that?" "Yes." "Now if He doesn't cast you out, what does He do?" "I suppose He takes me in." "Amen. Now He has taken you in and you are His child. Why don't you tell others about it?" So the bewildered seeker forces a

13

waxy smile and testifies that he has been converted to Christ. He is honest and means well but he has been led astray. He has fallen victim to a Spiritless logic. Such assurance as he has rests upon a shaky syllogism. There is no witness, no immediacy of knowledge, no encounter with God, no awareness of inner change.

Where there is a divine act within the soul there will always be a corresponding awareness. This act of God is self-validating. It is its own evidence and addresses itself direct to the religious consciousness. Abundant external evidence may exist that a work has been done within, and in this the reason may rejoice; but such evidence cannot be sufficient to guarantee that a saving work has been wrought. Whatever can be judged by reason is subject to the limitations and errors of reason. God waits to assure us that we are His children in a manner that eliminates the possibility of error, that is, by the inner witness.

In one of the most triumphant hymns ever written, "Arise, My Soul, Arise," by Charles Wesley, there occur these lines,

> *"His Spirit answers to the blood,*
> *And tells me I am born of God."*

To the salvation-by-logical-conclusion devotees such language is plain heresy. If it is heresy, I run to join such a glorious heretic. And may God send us many more.

14

Chapter 3

Faith Is a Journey, Not a Destination

"They continued stedfastly in the apostles' doctrine and fellowship, and in breaking of bread, and in prayers"—(ACTS 2:42).

So SAYS Luke of the thousands who received the Word and were baptized following the preaching of Peter on the day of Pentecost.

Conversion for those first Christians was not a destination; it was the beginning of a journey. And right there is where the Biblical emphasis differs from ours.

Today all is made to depend upon the initial act of believing. At a given moment a "decision" is made for Christ, and after that everything is automatic. This is not taught in so many words, but such is the impression inadvertently created by our failure to lay a scriptural emphasis in our evangelistic preaching. We of the evangelical churches are almost all guilty of this lopsided view of the Christian life, and because the foundations are out of plumb the temple of God leans dangerously and threatens to topple unless some immediate corrections are made.

In our eagerness to make converts we allow our hearers to absorb the idea that they can deal with their entire responsibility once and for all by an act of believing. This is in some vague way supposed to honor grace and glorify God, whereas actually it is to make Christ the author of a grotesque, unworkable system that has no counterpart in the Scriptures of truth.

In the Book of Acts faith was for each believer a beginning, not an end; it was a journey, not a bed in which to lie while waiting for the day of our Lord's triumph. Believing was not a once-done act; it was more than an act, it was an attitude of heart and mind which inspired and enabled the believer to take up his cross and follow the Lamb whithersoever He went.

"They continued," says Luke, and is it not plain that it was only by continuing that they could confirm their faith? On a given day they believed, were baptized and joined themselves to the believing company. Very good, but tomorrow what? and the next day? and the next week? How could anyone know that their conversion had been genuine? How could they live down the critic's charge that they had been pressured into a decision? that they had cracked under the psychological squeeze set up by crowds and religious excitement? Obviously there was only one way: They continued.

Not only did they continue, they continued steadfastly. So wrote Luke, and the word "steadfastly" is there to tell us that they continued against serious opposition. Steadfastness is required only when we are under attack, mental or physical, and the story of those early Christians is a story of faith under fire. The opposition was real.

Here again is seen the glaring discrepancy between Biblical Christianity and that of present-day evangelicals, particularly in the United States. In certain countries, I am told, some of our brethren are suffering painful persecution and counting not their lives dear unto themselves that they might win Christ. For these I have only utmost admiration. I speak not of such as they, but of the multitudes of religious weaklings within our evangelical fold here in America.

To make converts here we are forced to play down the difficulties and play up the peace of mind and worldly success enjoyed by those who accept Christ. We must assure our hearers that Christianity is now a proper and respectable thing and that Christ has become quite popular with political bigwigs, well-to-do business tycoons and the Hollywood swimming pool set. Thus assured, hell-deserving sinners are coming in droves to "accept" Christ for what they can get out of Him; and though one now and again may drop a tear as proof of his sincerity, it is hard to escape the conclusion that most of them are stooping to patronize the Lord of glory much as a young couple might fawn on a boresome but rich old uncle in order to be mentioned in his will later on.

We will never be completely honest with our hearers until we tell them the blunt truth that as

17

members of a race of moral rebels they are in a serious jam, and one they will not get out of easily. If they refuse to repent and believe on Christ they will most surely perish; if they do turn to Him, the same enemies that crucified Him will try to crucify them. One way they suffer alone without hope; the other way they suffer with Christ for a while, but in the midst of their suffering they enjoy His loving consolation and inward support and are able to rejoice even in tribulation.

Those first believers turned to Christ with the full understanding that they were espousing an unpopular cause that could cost them everything. They knew they would henceforth be members of a hated minority group with life and liberty always in jeopardy.

This is no idle flourish. Shortly after Pentecost some were jailed, many lost all their earthly goods, a few were slain outright and hundreds "scattered abroad."

They could have escaped all this by the simple expedient of denying their faith and turning back to the world; but this they steadfastly refused to do.

Seen thus in comparison with each other, is the Christianity of American evangelicalism today the same as that of the first century? I wonder. But again, I think I know.

Chapter 4

The Key to Human Life Is Theological

ANTHROPOLOGY TRIES to understand man by digging into his past and examining his primitive beginnings. Psychology seeks to understand him by digging into his mind. Philosophy takes whatever data it can assemble about man's external or internal life, past or present, borrows freely from historian and scientist, and reasons from this to the nature of man.

The answer to the question "What is man?" is sought by going straight to men to test and weigh and measure. Skull shape, bone structure, folklore, habits, customs, diet, superstitious practices, religion, social patterns, civil organization, tabus, reactions, emotions and countless other factors are taken into consideration in the search for the answer. The plan is, of course, to determine scientifically what man is by observing on a wide scale and over a long period what he does. But because the technique is wrong the conclusions must be false. It cannot be otherwise.

I well know that I am simply raising here the old question of naturalism versus supernaturalism, a question that has for centuries been fruitlessly debated and left unsettled for each generation to dispose of as it would or could. Were I a philosopher I might properly join the search for the key to life. As a man fully persuaded of the truth of the New Testament evangel and totally committed to Christ, there is for me no question here demanding an answer. That answer has been given in the positive and joyous Biblical declaration that God made man in His own image and likeness, akin to the earth as touching his physical body, it is true, but next of kin to heaven in his spirit, which came from God to return to God again (Eccl. 12:7). His body does not hold the key to his true nature; that key is found in his spirit which, while alienated from God by that mighty moral disaster theologians call the Fall, is yet susceptible of reclamation and full restoration to God through the redemption which is in Christ Jesus.

To know man we must begin with God. Secular learning, darkly colored as it is by humanism and rationalism in their various forms, has made a great many present-day Christians afraid to state their true position lest they earn for themselves one or more of the caustic sobriquets by which the wise men of this world stigmatize those who disagree with them; such, for instance, as "transcendentalist," "absolutist" or "supernaturalist."

As for myself, I do not fear such appellations even though they be hurled at me with the purpose of discrediting me once and for all. Far from fearing them, I glory in them. While I do not allow them to retain all the shades of meaning they have gathered to themselves in their journey down the years, I cheerfully accept them as far as they express meanings which I find in the Christian revelation.

No Christian, for instance, need draw back from the word "transcendentalist," for at the very root of his holy faith is belief in a transcendent world, a world above nature, different from and lying beyond matter and space and time, into which science cannot pry and at whose portals uncomprehending reason can do no other than reverently kneel and adore. Nor should he shrink from the word "supernaturalist," for it quite accurately describes an important tenet in his Christian creed. He does believe that there is a Divinity which shapes our ends. Nature, he holds, cannot account for herself but must humbly point upward to the One who gave her birth and whose invisible presence is her wisdom and her life. This he believes, and he considers everyone who believes less than this to be "finished and finite clods," Esaus who have sold their birthright for a mess of pottage.

Neither does the term "absolutist" make the instructed Christian blush or apologize. However scornfully the word may be spat at him, he is unperturbed. He knows his enemies are angry with him for refusing to accept two of their favorite doctrines, the relativity of morals and the pragmatic nature of religious beliefs. He does not try to deny that he holds with complete dogmatism the scriptural teaching that God is among other things uncreated, self-sufficient, eternal, infinite, sovereign and absolute. He glories in a

God absolutely holy, absolutely wise: in short, in a God who is everything that He is absolutely, unaffected by anything external to Himself. Indeed, it is necessary to him that he believe this about God; and if so to believe brands him as an absolutist he is quite happy about the whole thing. He knows what he believes, and words do not frighten him.

The flaw in current evangelism lies in its humanistic approach. It struggles to be supernaturalistic but never quite makes it. It is frankly fascinated by the great, noisy, aggressive world with its big names, its hero worship, its wealth and its garish pageantry. To the millions of disappointed persons who have always yearned for worldly glory but never attained to it, the modern evangel offers a quick and easy short cut to their heart's desire. Peace of mind, happiness, prosperity, social acceptance, publicity, success in sports, business, the entertainment field, and perchance to sit occasionally at the same banquet table with a celebrity—all this on earth and heaven at last. Certainly no insurance company can offer half as much.

In this quasi-Christian scheme of things God becomes the Aladdin lamp who does the bidding of everyone that will accept His Son and sign a card. The total obligation of the sinner is discharged when he accepts Christ. After that he has but to come with his basket and receive the religious equivalent of everything the world offers and enjoy it to the limit. Those who have not accepted Christ must be content with this world, but the Christian gets this one with the one to come thrown in as a bonus.

Such is the Christian message as interpreted by vast numbers of religious leaders today. This gross misapprehension of the truth is back of much (I almost said most) of our present evangelical activity. It determines directions, builds programs, decides the content of sermons, fixes the quality of local churches and even of whole denominations, sets the pattern for religious writers and forms the editorial policy of many evangelical publications.

This concept of Christianity is in radical error, and because it touches the souls of men it is a dangerous, even deadly, error. At bottom it is little more than weak humanism allied with weak Christianity to give it ecclesiastical respectability. It may be identified by its religious approach. Invariably it begins with man and his needs and then looks around for God; true Christianity reveals God as searching for man to deliver him from his ambitions.

Always and always God must be first. The gospel in its scriptural context puts the glory of God first and the salvation of man second. The angels, approaching from above, chanted, "Glory to God in the highest, and on earth peace, good will toward men." This puts the glory of God and the blessing of mankind in their proper order, as do also the opening words of the prayer, "Our Father which art in heaven, hallowed be thy name." Before any petitions are allowed, the name of God must be hallowed. God's glory is and must forever remain the Christian's true point of departure. Anything that begins anywhere else, whatever it is, is certainly not New Testament Christianity.

Chapter 5

The Power of God to Usward

"God hath spoken once: twice have I heard this; that power belongeth unto God"—(Psa. 62:11).

It is hard for us sons of the Machine Age to remember that there is no power apart from God. Whether physical, intellectual, moral or spiritual, power is contained in God, flows out from Him and returns to Him again. The power that works throughout His creation remains in Him even while it operates in an atom or a galaxy.

The notion that power is something God separates from Himself and tosses out to work apart from Him is erroneous. The power of nature is the Presence of God in His universe. This idea is woven into the Book of Job, the Wisdom books, the Psalms and the Prophets. The writings of John and Paul in the New Testament harmonize with this Old Testament doctrine, and in the Book of Hebrews it is said that Christ upholds all things by the word of His power.

We must not think of the power of God as a wild, irrational energy coursing haphazardly through the world like a lightning stroke or a tornado. This is the impression sometimes created by Bible teachers who keep reminding us that *dunamis,* the Greek word for power, is the root from which comes our word "dynamite." Little wonder that sensitive Christians shrink from contact with such a destructive and unpredictable force.

God is a Trinity in Unity. The undivided unity of the Godhead is a truth revealed to Israel and held unchanged by the Christian Church. The doctrine of the divine unity means not only that there is but one God; it means that the Triune God is one with Himself, of a single substance, without parts. This truth is celebrated by Faber in these lines,

Unfathomable Sea!
All life is out of Thee,
And Thy life is Thy blissful Unity.

All things that from Thee run,
All works that Thou hast done,
Thou didst in honor of Thy being One.

And by Thy being One,
Ever by that alone,
Couldst Thou do, and doest, what Thou hast done.

The power of God, then, is not something God has; it is something God is. Power is something that is true of God as wisdom and love are true of Him. It is, if we might so state it, a facet of His being, one with and indivisible from everything else that He is.

To imagine that the power of God operates blindly or accidentally is to fall victim to materialistic concepts. It is to think of God's power as separable from the attributes of personality such as wisdom, love and goodness. It is to imagine an infinite, undirected energy, something that does not and cannot exist.

The power of God is one with God's will, and works only as He wills that it should. It is one with His love and goodness and (as seen from our low standpoint) is the infinite enabling of all His attributes of perfection. It is His holy Being in action.

God is spirit and His universe is basically spiritual. Even science, which limps along far behind revelation, now knows that matter is not the solid, imporous substance it was once thought to be. Scientists change their beliefs radically from time to time and I do not want to quote them in confirmation of Christian truth; but there does appear to be a startling parallel between the atomic theory of matter and the Biblical concept of the Eternal Word as the source and support of all created things. Could it be that, as certain mystics have insisted, all things in heaven and on earth, visible and invisible, are in reality but the goings forth of the power of God?

Whatever God is He is infinitely. In Him lies all the power there is; any power at work anywhere is His. Even the power to do evil must first have come from Him since there is no other source from which it could come. Lucifer, son of the morning, when he lifted up himself against the Most High, had only the abilities he had received from God. These he misused to become the devil he is.

I am well aware that this kind of teaching raises certain very difficult questions, but we should never retreat before truth simply because we cannot explain it. To shrink from this truth is to raise still more and harder questions and, worst of all, it is to think feebly of God, the supreme indignity.

The fact of sin introduces a confusing element into our thinking about God and the universe, and requires that we suspend judgment on many things. Paul spoke of "the mystery of iniquity," and it becomes us to accept his inspired words as the only possible present answer to the question of sin. The wise man will note that the things we cannot understand have nothing to do with our salvation. We are saved by the truth we know.

If we are true Christians this we can know, that the boundless power of our infinite God is all around us, enfolding us, preserving us in being and keeping us unto salvation ready to be revealed. Let us look trustfully to God and expect "the working of his mighty power, which he wrought in Christ, when he raised him from the dead, and set him at his own right hand in the heavenly places" (Eph. 1:19, 20).

Chapter 6

We Live in a State of Emergency

THE FALL OF man has created a perpetual crisis. It will last until sin has been put down and Christ reigns over a redeemed and restored world.

Until that time the earth remains a disaster area and its inhabitants live in a state of extraordinary emergency.

· Statesmen and economists talk hopefully of "a return to normal conditions," but conditions have not been normal since "the woman saw that the tree was good for food . . . and pleasant" . . . and "to be desired to make one wise" and "took of the fruit thereof, and did eat, and gave also unto her husband with her; and he did eat."

It is not enough to say that we live in a state of moral crisis; that is true, but it is not all. To illustrate, we may say that war is a crisis in international relations, a breach of the peace between nations, but that is to leave much unsaid. Along with that breach comes widespread ruin, the death of countless thousands of human beings, the uprooting of families, indescribable mental and bodily suffering, the wanton destruction of property, hunger and disease and a hundred forms of misery which grow out of these other horrors and spread like fire over large portions of the earth, affecting millions of persons.

So the Fall was a moral crisis but it has affected every part of man's nature, moral, intellectual, psychological, spiritual and physical. His whole being has been deeply injured; the sin in his heart has overflowed into his total life, affecting his relation to God, to his fellow men and to everyone and everything that touches him.

There is also sound Bible reason to believe that nature itself, the brute creation, the earth and even the astronomical universe, have all felt the shock of man's sin and have been adversely affected by it.

When the Lord God drove out the man from the eastward garden and placed there cherubim and a flaming sword to prevent his return, the disaster was beginning to mount, and human history is little more than a record of its development.

It is not quite accurate to say that when our first parents fled from before the face of God they became fugitives and vagabonds in the earth; and it is certainly not true to say that they passed from the love and care of the One who had created them and against whom they had so deeply revolted. God never abandoned the creatures made in His image. Had they not sinned He would have cared for them by His presence; now He cares for them by His providence till a ransomed and regenerated people can look once more on His face (Rev. 21:3, 22:4).

Men are lost but not abandoned; that is what the Holy Scriptures teach and that is what the Church is commissioned to declare. The traveler lost in a blizzard knows he is lost; it is the assurance that a rescue party is searching for him that prevents his knowledge from turning to despair. His friends may not reach him in time, but the hope that they will enables him to stay alive when hunger and cold and shock say that he should die.

Let a flood or a fire hit a populous countryside and no able-bodied citizen feels that he has any right to rest till he has done all he can to save as many as he can. While death stalks farmhouse and village no one dares relax; this is the accepted code by which we live. The critical emergency for some becomes an emergency for all, from the highest government official to the local Boy Scout troop. As long as the flood rages or the fire roars on, no one talks of "normal times." No times are normal while helpless people cower in the path of destruction.

In times of extraordinary crisis ordinary measures will not suffice. The world lives in such a time of crisis. Christians alone are in a position to rescue the perishing. We dare not settle down to try to live as if things were "normal." Nothing is normal while sin and lust and death roam the world, pouncing upon one and another till the whole population has been destroyed.

To me it has always been difficult to understand those evangelical Christians who insist upon living in the crisis as if no crisis existed. They say they serve the Lord, but they divide their days so as to leave plenty of time to play and loaf and enjoy the pleasures of the world as well. They are at ease while the world burns; and they can furnish many convincing reasons for their conduct, even quoting Scripture if you press them a bit.

I wonder whether such Christians actually believe in the fall of man.

Chapter 7

Words Without Deeds: The Vice of Religion

IT WOULD BE a convenient arrangement were we so constituted that we could not talk better than we live.

For reasons known to God, however, there seems to be no necessary connection between our speaking and our doing; and here lies one of the deadliest snares in the religious life. I am afraid we modern Christians are long on talk and short on conduct. We use the language of power but our deeds are the deeds of weakness.

Our Lord and His apostles were long on deeds. The Gospels depict a Man walking in power, "who went about doing good, and healing all that were oppressed of the devil; for God was with him" (Acts 10:38). The moral relation between words and deeds appears quite plainly in the life and teachings of Christ. He did before He spoke and the doing gave validity to the speaking.

Luke wrote of "all that Jesus began both to do and teach," and I am sure that the order expressed there is not accidental. In the Sermon on the Mount Christ placed doing before teaching: "Whosoever therefore shall break one of these least commandments, and shall teach men so, he shall be called the least in the kingdom of heaven: but whosoever shall do and teach them, the same shall be called great in the kingdom of heaven" (Matt. 5:19).

Since in one of its aspects religion contemplates the invisible it is easy to understand how it can be erroneously made to contemplate the unreal. The praying man talks of that which he does not see, and fallen human minds tend to assume that what cannot be seen is not of any great importance, and probably not even real, if the truth were known. So religion is disengaged from practical life and retired to the airy region of fancy where dwell the sweet insubstantial nothings which everyone knows do not exist but which they nevertheless lack the courage to repudiate publicly.

I could wish that this were true only of pagan religions and of the vague and ill-defined quasi-religion of the average man; but candor dictates that I admit it to be true also of much that passes for evangelical Christianity in our times. Indeed it is more than possible that the gods of the heathen are more real to them than is the God of the average Christian. I sympathize with the mood of the poet Wordsworth when he wrote to the effect that he would rather be a sincere pagan who believed in a god that did not exist than to be a sophisticated Christian who disbelieved in a God who did.

Unquestionably there is not another institution in the world that talks as much and does as little as the church. Any factory that required as much raw material for so small a finished product would go bankrupt in six months. I have often thought that if one-tenth of one per cent of the prayers made in the churches of any ordinary American village on one Sunday were answered the country would be transformed overnight.

But that is just our trouble. We pour out millions of words and never notice that the prayers are not answered. I trust it may not be uncharitable to say that we not only do not expect our prayers to be answered but would be embarrassed or even disappointed if they were. I think it is not uncommon for Christians to present eloquent petitions to the Lord which they know will accomplish nothing, and some of those petitions they dare present only because they know that is the last they will hear of the whole thing. Many a wordy brother would withdraw his request quickly enough if he had any intimation that God was taking it seriously.

We settle for words in religion because deeds are too costly. It is easier to pray, "Lord, help me to carry my cross daily" than to pick up the cross and carry it; but since the mere request for help to do something we do not actually intend to do has a certain degree of religious comfort, we are content with repetition of the words.

The practice of substituting words for deeds is not something new. The apostle John saw symptoms of

34

it in his day and warned against it: "My little children, let us not love in word, neither in tongue; but in deed and in truth. And hereby we know that we are of the truth, and shall assure our hearts before him."

James also had something to say about the vice of words without deeds: "If a brother or sister be naked, and destitute of daily food, and one of you say unto them, Depart in peace, be ye warmed and filled; notwithstanding ye give them not those things which are needful to the body; what doth it profit?"

What then: Shall we take a vow of silence? Shall we cease to pray and sing and write and witness till we catch up on our deeds? No. That would not help. We Christians are left in the world to witness, and while we have breath we must speak to men about God and to God about men. How then shall we escape the snare of words without deeds?

It is simple, though not easy. First, let us say nothing we do not mean. Break the habit of conventional religious chatter. Speak only as we are ready to take the consequences. Believe God's promises and obey His commandments. Practice the truth and we may with propriety speak the truth. Deeds give body to words. As we do acts of power our words will take on authority and a new sense of reality will fill our hearts.

Chapter 8

The Erotic vs. the Spiritual

THE PERIOD IN which we now live may well go down in history as the Erotic Age. Sex love has been elevated into a cult. Eros has more worshipers among civilized men today than any other god. For millions the erotic has completely displaced the spiritual.

How the world got into this state is not difficult to trace. Contributing factors are the phonograph and radio, which can spread a love song from coast to coast within a matter of days; the motion picture and television, which enable a whole population to feast their eyes on sensuous women and amorous young men locked in passionate embrace (and this in the living rooms of "Christian" homes and before the eyes of innocent children!); shorter working hours and a multiplicity of mechanical gadgets with the resultant increased leisure for everyone. Add to these the scores of shrewdly contrived advertising campaigns which make sex the not too slyly concealed bait to attract buyers for almost every imaginable product;

the degraded columnists who have consecrated their lives to the task of the publicizing of soft, slinky nobodies with the faces of angels and the morals of alley cats; conscienceless novelists who win a doubtful fame and grow rich at the inglorious chore of dredging up literary putridities from the sewers of their souls to provide entertainment for the masses. These tell us something about how Eros has achieved his triumph over the civilized world.

Now if this god would let us Christians alone I for one would let his cult alone. The whole spongy, fetid mess will sink some day under its own weight and become excellent fuel for the fires of hell, a just recompense which is meet, and it becomes us to feel compassion for those who have been caught in its tragic collapse. Tears and silence might be better than words if things were slightly otherwise than they are. But the cult of Eros is seriously affecting the Church. The pure religion of Christ that flows like a crystal river from the heart of God is being polluted by the unclean waters that trickle from behind the altars of abomination that appear on every high hill and under every green tree from New York to Los Angeles.

The influence of the erotic spirit is felt almost everywhere in evangelical circles. Much of the singing in certain types of meetings has in it more of romance than it has of the Holy Ghost. Both words and music are designed to rouse the libidinous. Christ is courted with a familiarity that reveals a total ignorance of who He is. It is not the reverent intimacy of the adoring saint but the impudent familiarity of the carnal lover.

Religious fiction also makes use of sex to interest the reading public, the paper-thin excuse being that if romance and religion are woven into a story the average person who would not read a purely religious book will read the story and thus be exposed to the gospel. Leaving aside the fact that most modern religious novelists are home talent amateurs, scarcely one of whom is capable of writing a single line of even fair literature, the whole concept behind the religio-romantic novel is unsound. The libidinous impulses and the sweet, deep movings of the Holy Spirit are diametrically opposed to each other. The notion that Eros can be made to serve as an assistant of the Lord of glory is outrageous. The "Christian" film that seeks to draw customers by picturing amorous love scenes in its advertising is completely false to the religion of Christ. Only the spiritually blind will be taken in by it.

The current vogue of physical beauty and sparkling personalities in religious promotion is a further manifestation of the influence of the romantic spirit in the Church. The rhythmic sway, the synthetic smile and the too, too cheerful voice betray the religious worldling. He has learned his technique from the TV screen but not learned it well enough to succeed in the professional field, so he brings his inept production to the holy place and peddles it to the ailing and undersized Christians who are looking for something to amuse them while staying within the bounds of the current religious mores.

If my language should seem severe, let it be remembered that it is not directed at any individual. Toward the lost world of men I feel only a great compassion and a desire that all should come to repentance. For the Christians whose vigorous but mistaken leadership has wooed the modern church from the altar of Jehovah to the altars of error I feel genuine love and sympathy. I want to be the last to injure them and the first to forgive them, remembering my past sins and my need for mercy, as well as my own weakness and natural bent toward sin and error. Balaam's ass was used of God to rebuke a prophet. It would seem from this that God does not require perfection in the instrument He uses to warn and exhort His people.

When God's sheep are in danger the shepherd must not gaze at the stars and meditate on "inspirational" themes. He is morally obliged to grab his weapon and run to their defense. When the circumstances call for it, love can use the sword, though by her nature she would rather bind up the broken heart and minister to the wounded. It is time for the prophet and the seer to make themselves heard and felt again. For the last three decades timidity disguised as humility has crouched in her corner while the spiritual quality of evangelical Christianity has become progressively worse year by year. *How long, O Lord, how long?*

Chapter 9

What to Do About the Devil

HUMAN NATURE TENDS to excesses by a kind of evil magnetic attraction. We instinctively run to one of two extremes, and that is why we are so often in error.

A proof of this propensity to extremes is seen in the attitude of the average Christian toward the devil. I have observed among spiritual persons a tendency either to ignore him altogether or to make too much of him. Both are wrong.

There is in the world an enemy whom we dare not ignore. We see him first in the third chapter of Genesis and last in the twentieth of Revelation; which is to say that he was present at the beginning of human history and will be there at its earthly close.

This enemy is not a creation of religious fancy, not a mere personification of evil for convenience, but a being as real as man himself. The Bible attributes to him qualities of personality too detailed to be figurative, and reveals him speaking and acting in situations hard and practical and far removed from the poetic imagination.

The devil is declared in the Scriptures to be an enemy of God and of all good men. He is said to be a liar, a deceiver and a murderer who achieves his ends by guile and trickery. Because he is a spirit he is able to "walk up and down in the earth" at his pleasure. While he is not omnipresent (omnipresence being an attribute of God alone) he is ubiquitous, which for his purpose amounts to the same thing.

The enemy bears many names, among them being the dragon, the serpent, the devil and Satan. In addition to this one supreme evil being there are demons, "principalities," "powers," "rulers of the darkness of this world" and "wicked spirits in high places" which operate under his direction. How successful this band of cosmic outlaws has been is written into human history with a pen dipped in blood. The havoc they have wrought in the earth is so frightful as to exceed all power of description. Every newspaper, every news broadcast is a proof of the existence of that evil genius called the devil and his band of vicious spirits dedicated to destruction.

Satan hates God for His own sake, and everything that is dear to God he hates for the very reason that God loves it. Because man was made in God's image the hatred with which Satan regards him is particularly malevolent, and since the Christian is doubly dear to God he is hated by the powers of darkness with an aggravated fury probably not equaled anywhere else in the moral universe.

In view of this it cannot be less than folly for us Christians to disregard the reality and presence of the enemy. To live in a world under siege is to live in constant peril; to live there and be wholly unaware of the peril is to increase it a hundredfold and to turn the world into a paradise for fools.

While we must not underestimate the strength of the foe, we must at the same time be careful not to fall under his evil spell and live in constant fear of him. "We are not ignorant of his devices." If he cannot make skeptics of us he will make us devil-conscious and thus throw a permanent shadow across our lives. There is but a hairline between truth and superstition. We should learn the truth about the enemy, but we must stand bravely against every superstitious notion he would introduce about himself. The truth will set us free but superstition will enslave us.

I know Christians so engrossed with the fight against evil spirits that they are in a state of constant turmoil. Their touching effort to hold the devil at bay exhausts them nervously and physically, and they manage to stay alive only by frantically calling on God and rebuking the devil in the name of Christ. These are innocent spiritists in reverse and are devil-conscious to a point of being borderline neurotics. They grow sensitive and suspicious and always manage to locate an evil spirit as the cause back of everything that irritates them; then their hackles stand straight up and they begin to order the devil about in a loud voice, but their nervous gestures tell how deeply frightened they are.

The bad thing about all this is that it is contagious and will soon turn a joyous, worshipful congregation into a crowd of scared and jumpy persons, nervous and completely unhappy.

The scriptural way to see things is to set the Lord always before us, put Christ in the center of our vision, and if Satan is lurking around he will appear on the margin only and be seen as but a shadow on the edge of the brightness. It is always wrong to reverse this —to set Satan in the focus of our vision and push God out to the margin. Nothing but tragedy can come of such inversion.

The best way to keep the enemy out is to keep Christ in. The sheep need not be terrified by the wolf; they have but to stay close to the shepherd. It is not the praying sheep Satan fears but the presence of the shepherd.

The instructed Christian whose faculties have been developed by the Word and the Spirit will not fear the devil. When necessary he will stand against the powers of darkness and overcome them by the blood of the Lamb and the word of his testimony. He will recognize the peril in which he lives and will know what to do about it, but he will practice the presence of God and never allow himself to become devil-conscious.

Chapter 10

To Be Right,
We Must Think Right

WHAT WE THINK about when we are free to think
about what we will—that is what we are or will soon
become.

The Bible has a great deal to say about our
thoughts; current evangelicalism has practically nothing to say about them. The reason the Bible says so
much is that our thoughts are so vitally important to
us; the reason evangelicalism says so little is that we
are over-reacting from the "thought" cults, such as
New Thought, Unity, Christian Science and their like.
These cults make our thoughts to be very nearly
everything and we counter by making them very
nearly nothing. Both positions are wrong.

Our voluntary thoughts not only reveal what we
are, they predict what we will become. Except for
that conduct which springs from our basic natural
instincts, all conscious behavior is preceded by and
arises out of our thoughts. The will can become a
servant of the thoughts, and to a large degree even

44

our emotions follow our thinking. "The more I think about it the madder I get" is the way the average man states it, and in so doing not only reports accurately on his own mental processes but pays as well an unconscious tribute to the power of thought. Thinking stirs feeling and feeling triggers action. That is the way we are made and we may as well accept it.

The Psalms and Prophets contain numerous references to the power of right thinking to raise religious feeling and incite to right conduct. "I thought on my ways, and turned my feet unto thy testimonies." "While I was musing the fire burned: then spake I with my tongue." Over and over the Old Testament writers exhort us to get quiet and think about high and holy things as a preliminary to amendment of life or a good deed or a courageous act.

The Old Testament is not alone in its respect for the God-given power of human thought. Christ taught that men defile themselves by evil thinking and even went so far as to equate a thought with an act: "Whosoever looketh on a woman to lust after her hath committed adultery with her already in his heart." Paul recited a list of shining virtues and commanded, "Think on these things."

These quotations are but four out of hundreds that could be cited from the Scriptures. Thinking about God and holy things creates a moral climate favorable to the growth of faith and love and humility and reverence. We cannot by thinking regenerate our hearts, nor take our sins away nor change the leopard's spots. Neither can we by thinking add one cubit to our stature or make evil good or darkness light. So to teach is to misrepresent a scriptural truth and to use it to our own undoing. But we can by Spirit-inspired thinking help to make our minds pure sanctuaries in which God will be pleased to dwell.

I referred in a previous paragraph to "our voluntary thoughts" and I used the words advisedly. In our journey through this evil and hostile world many thoughts will be forced upon us which we do not like and for which we have no moral sympathy. The necessity to make a living may compel us for days on end to entertain thoughts in no sense elevating. Ordinary awareness of the doings of our fellow men will bring thoughts repugnant to our Christian soul. These need affect us but little. For them we are not responsible and they may pass through our minds like a bird through the air, without leaving a trace. They have no lasting effect upon us because they are not our own. They are unwelcome intruders for which we have no love and which we get rid of as quickly as possible.

Anyone who wishes to check on his true spiritual condition may do so by noting what his voluntary thoughts have been over the last hours or days. What has he thought about when free to think of what he pleased? Toward what has his inner heart turned when it was free to turn where it would? When the bird of thought was let go did it fly out like the raven to settle upon floating carcasses or did it like the dove circle and return again to the ark of God? Such a test is easy to run, and if we are honest with ourselves we can discover not only what we are but what we are going to become. We'll soon be the sum of our voluntary thoughts.

While our thoughts stir our feelings, and thus strongly influence our wills, it is yet true that the will can be and should be master of our thoughts. Every normal person can determine what he will think about. Of course the troubled or tempted man may find his thoughts somewhat difficult to control and even while he is concentrating upon a worthy object, wild and fugitive thoughts may play over his mind like heat lightning on a summer evening. These are likely to be more bothersome than harmful and in the long run do not make much difference one way or another.

The best way to control our thoughts is to offer the mind to God in complete surrender. The Holy Spirit will accept it and take control of it immediately. Then it will be relatively easy to think on spiritual things, especially if we train our thought by long periods of daily prayer. Long practice in the art of mental prayer (that is, talking to God inwardly as we work or travel) will help to form the habit of holy thought.

Chapter 11

The Way of True Greatness

"*Whosoever will be great among you, let him be your minister*," said our Lord—(MATT. 20:20-28), and from these words we may properly conclude (and the context strongly supports the conclusion) that there is nothing wrong with the desire to be great provided (1) we seek the right kind of greatness; (2) we allow God to decide what is greatness; (3) we are willing to pay the full price that greatness demands, and (4) we are content to wait for the judgment of God to settle the whole matter of who is great at last.

It is vitally important, however, that we know what Christ meant when He used the word *great* in relation to men, and His meaning cannot be found in the lexicon or dictionary. Only when viewed in its broad theological setting is it understood aright. No one whose heart has had a vision of God, however brief or imperfect that vision may have been, will ever consent to think of himself or anyone else as being great. The sight of God, when He appears in awesome majesty to the wondering eyes of the soul, will bring the worshiper to his knees in fear and gladness and fill him with such an overwhelming sense of divine greatness that he must spontaneously cry "Only God is great!"

All this being true, still God Himself applies the word great to men, as when the angel tells Zacharias that the son who is to be born "shall be great in the sight of the Lord," or as when Christ speaks of some who shall be great in the kingdom of heaven.

Obviously there are two kinds of greatness recognized in the Scriptures—an absolute, uncreated greatness belonging to God alone, and a relative and finite greatness achieved by or bestowed upon certain friends of God and sons of faith who by obedience and self-denial sought to become as much like God as possible. It is of this latter kind of greatness that we speak.

To seek greatness is not wrong in itself. Men were once made in the image of God and told to subdue the earth and have dominion. Man's very desire to rise above his present state and to bring all things under subjection to him may easily be the blind impulse of his fallen nature to fulfill the purpose for which he was created. Sin has perverted this natural instinct as it has all others. Men have left their first estate and in their moral ignorance invariably look for greatness where it is not and seek to attain it in ways that are always vain and often downright iniquitous.

By the life He lived and the words He spoke our Lord cleared up the confusion that existed concerning human greatness. That is, He cleared it up for all who are willing to hear His words and to accept His life as a model for their own.

The essence of His teaching is that true greatness lies in character, not in ability or position. Men in their blindness had always thought that superior talents made a man great, and so the vast majority believe today. To be endowed with unusual abilities in the field of art or literature or music or statecraft, for instance, is thought to be in itself an evidence of greatness, and the man thus endowed is hailed as a great man. Christ taught, and by His life demonstrated, that greatness lies deeper.

"The princes of the Gentiles," He called the men who gained political power by their superior talents or who inherited their position of dominion over their fellow men. It is obvious that He was not impressed by that kind of greatness, for He drew a sharp line between it and true greatness. "It shall not be so among you," He told His followers. A new and radical conception of greatness had been introduced.

While a few philosophers and religionists of pre-Christian times had seen the fallacy in man's idea of greatness and had exposed it, it was Christ who located true greatness and showed how it could be attained. "Whosoever will be great among you, let him be your minister; and whosoever will be chief among you, let him be your servant." It is that simple and that easy—and that difficult.

The ease and the simplicity are there for anyone to see. We have but to follow Christ in service to the human race, a selfless service that asks only to serve, and greatness will be ours. That is all, but it is too much, for it runs counter to all that is Adam in us. Adam still feels the instinct for dominion; he hears deep within him the command: "Replenish the earth, and subdue it," and he does not take kindly to the command to serve. And there lies the confusion, the contradiction, that sin has brought, for sin is the trouble after all, and sin must go.

Sin must go and Adam must give way to Christ; so says our Lord in effect. By sin men have lost dominion, even their very right to it, until they win it back by humble service. Though redeemed from death and hell by the vicarious labor of Christ on the cross, still the right to have dominion must be won by each man separately. Each must fulfill a long apprenticeship as a servant before he is fit to rule.

After Christ had served (and His service included death) God highly exalted Him and gave Him a name above every name. As a man He served and won His right to have dominion.

Christ found it easy to serve because He had no sin. Nothing in Him rebelled against the lowliest ministrations our fallen nature required. He knew where true greatness lay and we do not. We try to climb up to high position when God has ordained that we go down. "Whosoever will be chief among you, let him be your servant."

Chapter 12

Heard but by Our Singing

THE DESIRE TO BE held in esteem by our fellow men is universal and as natural to us as is the instinct for self-preservation.

The Bible recognizes this inborn desire and, contrary to what we might expect, not only does not condemn it but actually appeals to it on occasion. "A good name is rather to be chosen than great riches," says the wise man, and the apostle Paul spoke frankly of the esteem in which certain persons and churches were held and used it as a stimulant to good living on the part of others. We refer to this quality in human nature when we say of a man who has ceased to care what people think of him that he has "lost his self-respect."

We may properly conclude that it is right and natural that we should value the approbation of society. It is a measure of our love for men that we should want them to love us. There is an unrealistic humility which would have it otherwise, but I believe the truth is as stated here.

The cross would not be a cross to us if it destroyed in us only the unreal and the artificial. It is when it goes on to slay the best in us that its cruel sharpness is felt. If it slew only our sins it might be bearable, even kind, as the knife of the surgeon is kind when it removes the foreign matter that would take our lives if allowed to remain; but when we must suffer the loss of things both precious and good, then we taste the bitterness of the nails and the thorns.

To value the esteem of mankind and for Christ's sake to renounce it is a form of crucifixion suffered by true Christians since the days of the apostles. For it cannot be denied that the way of the cross is unpopular and that it brings a measure of reproach upon those who take it. It is rare that a separated Christian escapes a certain odium in his lifetime. After he has been dead a long while, time and distance may soften the lines of the portrait and the world that hated him while he lived will often praise him when he is gone.

John Wesley and his Methodists are good examples of this strange phenomenon. They were scorned and derided while they walked on earth; offscourings they were, to be persecuted or, worse, to be let coldly alone as if they were lepers. Now we sing their hymns and build their sepulchres, but history has recorded the abuses once heaped upon them for their "perfectionism" and for that irrepressible joy of theirs that embarrassed people and made them look away and hurry out of their presence.

Gerhard Tersteegen, whom I never tire of quoting, in a lovely little hymn called "Pilgrim Song," seeks to comfort and cheer the holy wayfarers passing unloved and unnoticed through the wilderness. The last stanza reads,

> We follow in His footsteps;
>   What if our feet be torn?
> Where He has marked the pathway
>   All hail the briar and thorn!
> Scarce seen, scarce heard, unreckoned,
>   Despised, defamed, unknown
> Or heard but by our singing,
>   On, children! ever on!

The line "Or heard but by our singing" has in it more of the true spirit of church history than all the large tomes ever written. The learned historians tell of councils and bulls and religious wars, but in the midst of all the mummery were a few who saw the Eternal City in full view and managed almost to walk on earth as if they had already gone to he .ven. These were the joyous ones who got little recognition from the world of institutionalized religion, and might have gone altogether unnoticed except for their singing.

Unsung but singing: this is the short and simple story of many today whose names are not known beyond the small circle of their own small company. Their gifts are not many nor great, but their song is sweet and clear.

John Milton lost his sight and mourned that loss in beautiful and touching verse in the third book of his *Paradise Lost*. Night had settled all about him, he sighed, and never again would he see

> *Day, or the sweet approach of even or morn,*
> *Or sight of vernal bloom, or summer's rose,*
> *Or flocks, or herds, or human face divine.*

But in spite of his affliction he refused to be desolate. If he could not see, he could still think and he could still pray; and he could listen to his own heart, he said, and move "harmonious numbers." Like the nightingale he could sing in the darkness

> *. . . as the wakeful bird*
> *Sings darkling, and, in shadiest covert hid,*
> *Tunes her nocturnal note.*

Well, the world is big and tangled and dark, and we are never sure where a true Christian may be found. One thing we do know: the more like Christ he is the less likely it will be that a newspaper reporter will be seeking him out. However much he may value the esteem of his fellow men, he may for the time be forced to stand under the shadow of their displeasure. Or the busy world may actually not even know he is there—except that they hear him singing.

Chapter 13

Faith Dares to Fail

IN THIS WORLD MEN are judged by their ability to do.

They are rated according to the distance they have come up the hill of achievement. At the bottom is utter failure; at the top complete success, and between these two extremes the majority of civilized men sweat and struggle from youth to old age.

A few give up, slide to the bottom and become inhabitants of Skid Row. There, with ambition gone and will broken, they subsist on handouts till nature forecloses on them and death takes them away.

At the top are the few who by a combination of talent, hard work and good fortune manage to reach the peak and all the luxury, fame and power that are found there.

But in all of this there is no happiness. The effort to succeed puts too much strain on the nerves. Excessive preoccupation with the struggle to win narrows the mind, hardens the heart and shuts out a thousand bright visions which might be enjoyed if there were only leisure to notice them.

The man who reaches the pinnacle is seldom happy for very long. He soon becomes eaten by fears that he may slip back a peg and be forced to surrender his place to another. Examples of this are found in the feverish way the TV star watches his rating and the politician his mail.

Let an elected official learn that a poll shows him to be two per cent less popular in August than he was in March and he begins to sweat like a man on his way to prison. The ball player lives by his averages, the businessman by his rising graph and the concert star by his applause meter. It is not uncommon for a challenger in the ring to weep openly when he fails to knock out the champion. To be second best leaves him completely disconsolate; he must be first to be happy.

This mania to succeed is a good thing perverted. The desire to fulfill the purpose for which we were created is of course a gift from God, but sin has twisted this impulse about and turned it into a selfish lust for first place and top honors. By this lust the whole world of mankind is driven as by a demon, and there is no escape.

When we come to Christ we enter a different world. The New Testament introduces us to a spiritual philosophy infinitely higher than and altogether contrary to that which motivates the world. According to the teaching of Christ the poor in spirit are blessed; the meek inherit the earth; the first are last and the last first; the greatest man is the one that best serves others; the one who loses everything is the only one that will have everything at last; the successful man of the world will see his hoarded treasures swept away by the tempest of judgment; the righteous beggar goes to Abraham's bosom and the rich man burns in the fires of hell.

Our Lord died an apparent failure, discredited by the leaders of established religion, rejected by society and forsaken by His friends. The man who ordered Him to the cross was the successful statesman whose hand the ambitious hack politician kissed. It took the resurrection to demonstrate how gloriously Christ had triumphed and how tragically the governor had failed.

Yet today the professed church seems to have learned nothing. We are still seeing as men see and judging after the manner of man's judgment. How much eager-beaver religious work is done out of a carnal desire to make good. How many hours of prayer are wasted beseeching God to bless projects that are geared to the glorification of little men. How much sacred money is poured out upon men who, in spite of their tear-in-the-voice appeals, nevertheless seek only to make a fair show in the flesh.

The true Christian should turn away from all this. Especially should ministers of the gospel search their own hearts and look deep into their inner motives. No man is worthy to succeed until he is willing to fail. No man is morally worthy of success in religious activities until he is willing that the honor of succeeding should go to another if God so wills.

God may allow His servant to succeed when He has disciplined him to a point where he does not need to succeed to be happy. The man who is elated by success and cast down by failure is still a carnal man. At best his fruit will have a worm in it.

God will allow His servant to succeed when he has learned that success does not make him dearer to God nor more valuable in the total scheme of things. We cannot buy God's favor with crowds or converts or new missionaries sent out or Bibles distributed. All these things can be accomplished without the help of the Holy Spirit. A good personality and a shrewd knowledge of human nature is all that any man needs to be a success in religious circles today.

Our great honor lies in being just what Jesus was and is. To be accepted by those who accept Him, rejected by all who reject Him, loved by those who love Him and hated by everyone that hates Him. What greater glory could come to any man?

We can afford to follow Him to failure. Faith dares to fail. The resurrection and the judgment will demonstrate before all worlds who won and who lost. We can wait.

Chapter 14

Light Requires Sight

To FIND THE WAY we need more than light; we need also sight.

The Holy Scriptures are the source of moral and spiritual light. "The entrance of thy words giveth light," says the psalmist; and again, "Thy word is a lamp unto my feet, and a light unto my path."

I believe in the plenary inspiration of the Scriptures as originally given, and I can sing with the hymnist,

> "We praise Thee for the radiance
>   That from the hallowed page,
> A lantern to our footsteps,
>   Shines on from age to age."

Yet I consider that I cast no aspersion upon the hallowed page when I say that its radiance is not by itself enough. Light alone is not sufficient.

Light is a figure which the Bible and religious teachers often use when they mean knowledge. As long as men do not know, they are said to be in darkness. The coming of knowledge is like the rising of the sun. But sunrise means nothing to the unseeing eye. Only the sighted benefit from the light of the sun.

Between light and sight there is a wide difference. One man may have light without sight; he is blind. Another may have sight without light; he is temporarily blind, but the coming of the light quickly enables him to see. The Philippian jailer had good eyes, but he "called for a light" in order to find Paul in the darkness. But all the light of the sun, moon and stars could not help poor Samson, for the Philistines had bored out his eyes.

It is always night to a blind man, and it is always day to the man with a lantern—provided he can see. A couplet from the Hindu Book of Good Counsel points this up:

> *"Though a blind man hold a lantern,*
> *Yet his footsteps stray aside."*

What does all this say to us? Simply that religious instruction, however sound, is not enough by itself. It brings light, but it cannot impart sight. The text without the Spirit's enlightenment cannot save the sinner. Salvation follows a work of the Spirit in the heart. There can be no salvation apart from truth but there can be, and often is, truth without salvation. How many multiplied thousands have learned the catechism by heart and still wander in moral darkness because there has been no inward illumination.

The assumption that light and sight are synonymous has brought spiritual tragedy to millions. A blind man may face a beautiful landscape with eyes wide open and see nothing; and a blind heart may hear saving truth and understand nothing. The Pharisees looked straight at the Light of the World for three years, but not one ray of light reached their inner beings. Light is not enough.

The disciples of Jesus were instructed in the Scriptures. Christ Himself had taught them out of the law of Moses and the prophets and the psalms; yet it took a specific act of inward "opening" before they could grasp the truth. "Then opened he their understanding, that they might understand the scriptures" (Luke 24:45). When Paul preached at Philippi a certain woman named Lydia heard, believed, was baptized and immediately put her house at Paul's disposal. But one highly significant little phrase explains the whole thing: "whose heart the Lord opened" (Acts 16:14). Lydia received sight as well as light.

The apostle discovered very early in his ministry that, as he put it, "not all men have faith." And he knew why. "But if our gospel be hid, it is hid to them that are lost: in whom the god of this world hath blinded the minds of them which believe not, lest the light of the glorious gospel of Christ, who is the image of God, should shine unto them" (2 Cor. 4:3, 4).

Satan has no fear of the light as long as he can keep his victims sightless. The uncomprehending mind is unaffected by truth. The intellect of the hearer may grasp saving knowledge while yet the heart makes no moral response to it. A classic example of this is seen in the story of Benjamin Franklin and George Whitefield. In his autobiography Franklin recounts in some detail how he listened to the mighty preaching of the great evangelist. He even walked around the square where Whitefield stood to learn for himself how far that golden voice carried. Whitefield talked with Franklin personally about his need of Christ and promised to pray for him. Years later Franklin wrote rather sadly that the evangelist's prayers must not have done any good, for he was still unconverted.

No one could doubt the intellectual brilliance of Franklin and certainly Whitefield preached the whole truth; yet nothing came of it. Why? The only answer is that Franklin had light without sight. He never saw the Light of the World. To do this requires an act of inward enlightenment wrought by the Spirit, something which Franklin apparently never received.

The inward operation of the Holy Spirit is necessary to saving faith. The gospel is light but only the Spirit can give sight. When seeking to bring the lost to Christ we must pray continually that they may receive the gift of seeing. And we must pit our prayer against that dark spirit who blinds the hearts of men.

Chapter 15

Accepting the Universe

WHEN CARLYLE HEARD that Margaret Fuller had decided to "accept the universe" he roared with laughter. "Well, she'd better!" he shouted good-naturedly. And she had. And so had we.

This idea was once expressed better by a simplehearted man who was asked how he managed to live in such a state of constant tranquility even though surrounded by circumstances anything but pleasant. His answer was as profound as it was simple: "I have learned," he said, "to coöperate with the inevitable."

The idea here set forth is so wise and practical that it is hard to see how we Christians have managed to overlook it so completely in our everyday living. That we do overlook it is shown by our conduct and conversation. Some of us "kick against the pricks" for a lifetime, all the while believing that we are surrendered to the will of God.

Some of the Stoic moral philosophers appear to have known more about this secret than many Christians do. Epictetus, for instance, would never dream of resenting circumstances or complaining about his lot in life. To do so would be to rebel against God. According to his teaching, men are placed in a world over which they have no control and are therefore not accountable to God for the direction the world takes. What wicked men do should not disturb the good man's tranquility. These things belong to the world outside. It is the inner world that matters, because that is the only world over which we have control and the only one for which we shall be held responsible. The inner world consists of our thoughts and emotions, presided over by our will. While we cannot determine circumstances we can determine our reaction to them. And there is where the battle is to be fought and the victory won.

This is not to teach fatalism or to deny the freedom of the human will. Quite the contrary, it is to assert that freedom unequivocally. Though we cannot control the universe, we can determine our attitude toward it. We can accept God's will wherever it is expressed and take toward it an attitude of worshipful resignation. If my will is to do God's will, then there will be no controversy with anything that comes in the course of my daily walk. Inclement weather, unpleasant neighbors, physical handicaps, adverse political conditions—all these will be accepted as God's will for the time and surrendered to provisionally, subject to such alterations as God may see fit to make, either by His own sovereign providence or in answer to believing prayer.

To "accept the universe" does not mean that we are to accept evil conditions as inevitable and make no effort to improve them. So to teach would be to cancel the plain teachings of the Scriptures on that point. Where a situation is contrary to the will of God, and there are clear promises concerning it in the Scriptures, it is our privilege and obligation to pray and labor to bring about a change. Should we become ill, for instance, we should not surrender to the illness as being inevitable and do nothing about it. Rather we should accept it provisionally as the will of God for the time and seek His will about recovering our health. The big thing, however, is that we do not chafe against our illness and resist it as something that has visited us outside the will of God. Or if a fair examination of the facts proves that our illness was caused by some disobedience to the plain commandments of the Scriptures, we have but to confess it and make whatever amendments are indicated in the Word. This will bring us back into the center of God's will and put our lives on course. But to fret and complain against our afflictions like an animal caught in a trap is to miss the whole disciplinary purpose of God in our lives. God will heal and alter conditions but He will not do so for fretful souls who chew at the trap of circumstances and pity themselves for their sufferings.

While the prayer of faith enables us to lay hold of the omnipotence of God and bring about many wonderful changes here below, there are some things that not even prayer can change. These lie outside the field of prayer and must be accepted with thanksgiving as the wise will of God for us.

We should, for instance, accept the wisdom of God in nature. In the course of a lifetime there may be a thousand things we could wish had been different, but the word *wish* is not in the Christian's vocabulary. The very word connotes a fretful rebellion against the ways of God in His universe. Let's accept that universe.

Again, accept yourself. Apart from sin, which you have forsaken and which you mean to practice no more, there is nothing about yourself of which you need be ashamed. That you are who you are and what you are; that you were born of your particular hereditary line; that you are of your particular sex, race, color, size; that you were born into these times and not into some other period in history—for these things thank God sincerely and accept your divinely appointed status. Cease to vex yourself about anything over which you have no control. Keep your heart with all diligence and God will look after the universe. It's remarkable what peace this simple spiritual philosophy will bring to the soul.

Chapter 16

Sanctifying the Ordinary

A CHRISTIAN POET of a bygone generation wrote a rather long hymn around a single idea: You can, by three little words, turn every common act of your life into an offering acceptable to God. The words are *"For Thy sake."*

The hymn is no longer familiar to the Christian public. Its form is rather old-fashioned and its mood foreign to the psychology of the busy believers who scurry about so nervously these days. Scarcely one in ten thousand of them would have the patience to read it if it were placed in their hands; yet its simple message is so wonderful that it should never be allowed to be lost. Rather it should be rescued from oblivion and given back to the sons of the kingdom as a precious treasure they can ill afford longer to neglect.

Today more than ever we Christians need to learn how to sanctify the ordinary. This is a blasé generation. People have been overstimulated to the place where their nerves are jaded and their tastes corrupted. Natural things have been rejected to make room for things artificial. The sacred has been secularized, the holy vulgarized and worship converted into a form of entertainment. A dopey, blear-eyed generation seeks constantly for some new excitement powerful enough to bring a thrill to its worn-out and benumbed sensibilities. So many wonders have been discovered or invented that nothing on earth is any longer wonderful. Everything is common and almost everything boring.

Like it or not, that is the world in which we find ourselves and we are charged with the responsibility to live soberly, righteously and godly right in the middle of it. The danger is that we allow ourselves to be too much affected by the degenerate tastes and low views of the Hittites and Jebusites among whom we dwell and so learn the ways of the nations, to our own undoing, as Israel did before us.

When the whole moral and psychological atmosphere is secular and common how can we escape its deadly effects? How can we sanctify the ordinary and find true spiritual meaning in the common things of life? The answer has already been suggested. It is to consecrate the whole of life to Christ and begin to do everything in His name and for His sake.

Fénelon teaches that to make our deeds acceptable to God it is not necessary that we change our occupation (if it is honest), but only that we begin to do for Christ's sake what we had formerly been doing for our own. To some of us this will seem too tame and ordinary. We want to do great things for God, to hazard our lives in dramatic acts of devotion that will attract the attention of fellow Christians and perhaps of the larger world outside. Visions of Huss at the stake, Luther at the Diet of Worms or Livingstone in the heart of Africa flit before our minds as we think on spiritual things. Plain, workaday Christians like us— how can we rise to such heroic heights? With our families to support, with our lot cast in the dull routine of the commonplace, with no one threatening us with imprisonment or death: how can we live lives acceptable to God? What can we do to satisfy the heart of our Father in heaven?

The answer is near thee, even in thy mouth. Vacate the throne room of your heart and enthrone Jesus there. Set Him in the focus of your heart's attention and stop wanting to be a hero. Make Him your all in all and try yourself to become less and less. Dedicate your entire life to His honor alone and shift the motives of your life from self to God. Let the reason back of your daily conduct be Christ and His glory, not yourself, nor your family nor your country nor your church. In all things let Him have the preëminence.

All this seems too simple to be true, but Scripture and experience agree to declare that it is indeed the way to sanctify the ordinary. "For Thy sake" will rescue the little, empty things from vanity and give them eternal meaning. The lowly paths of routine living will by these words be elevated to the level of a bright highway. The humdrum of our daily lives will take on the quality of a worship service and the thousand irksome duties we must perform will become offerings and sacrifices acceptable to God by Christ Jesus.

To God there are no small offerings if they are made in the name of His Son. Conversely, nothing appears great to Him that is given for any other reason than for Jesus' sake. If we cannot die for Christ we can live for Him, and sometimes this is more heroic and will bring a larger reward.

"For Thy sake." These are the wondrous words which, when they are found in the heart as well as in the mouth, turn water into wine and every base metal into gold.

Chapter 17

Quality Matters, Not Size

To God quality is vastly important and size matters little. When set in opposition to size, quality is everything and size nothing.

This is not hard to understand, seeing that size is a creature-word and applies to matter only. It has to do with dimension, weight or number of things created. God has no size, for the obvious reason that none of the attributes of matter apply to Him and size is an attribute of matter.

To attribute size to God is to make Him subject to degrees, which He can never be, seeing that the very idea of degree relates to created things only. That which is infinite cannot be greater or less, larger or smaller, and God is infinite. God simply is without qualification. "I AM THAT I AM" is how He in condescending patience accounts to created intelligence for His uncreated Being.

Quality, as the word is used here, has to do with pure being, with intrinsicality, and does not properly admit of degree. For this reason we may attribute quality to God, but not size.

God made man in His own image and gave him intellect, emotion and will along with moral perception and the ability to know and worship his Creator. These attributes constitute quality of being and differentiate the man from the world around him and even from his own body. Material bodies have extension in space, weight and form, but they lack the ability to think or feel or love or yearn or worship. Because they lack this ability, and especially because they lack the power of will, they possess no moral or spiritual qualities whatsoever; and because they have not such qualities they are nothing in themselves, their only significance being that which may for the moment be lent them by God or by the man He made in his own likeness.

Man's moral fall has clouded his vision, confused his thinking and rendered him subject to delusion. One evidence of this is his all but incurable proneness to confuse values and put size before quality in his appraisal of things. The Christian faith reverses this order, but even Christians tend to judge things by the old Adamic rule. How big? How much? and How many? are the questions oftenest asked by religious persons when trying to evaluate Christian things. This is done by a kind of unconscious reflex, because in the world of matter, motion, space and time these questions have valid meaning. In the world of spirit they have no meaning at all, and yet we carry them over into the kingdom of God, evidence enough that our minds have been but imperfectly renewed.

Our problem is that we think as men. We savor not of heaven but of earth, and our psychology is not that of Christ but that of Adam. All the while we stubbornly insist that we are evangelicals, but it is to our shame that many of the pagan philosophers were more spiritual-minded than we. Socrates, Epictetus, Marcus Aurelius and a great many more could be brought forward to witness against us. They were wiser in their generation without the light of the New Testament than we are with that light.

The Christian faith engages a spiritual kingdom where quality of being is everything. "The hour cometh, and now is, when the true worshippers shall worship the Father in spirit and in truth: for the Father seeketh such to worship him. God is a Spirit: and they that worship him must worship him in spirit and in truth." With these words Jesus showed how far both Jews and Samaritans were astray in their argument over the proper place to worship. Not the beauty of a city nor the size of a mountain matters to the Father; truth and spirit and all the wealth of moral qualities that gather around them: these are all in all.

It is not uncommon to find college students whose faith in Christ has been badly shaken by their exposure to teachings of science. After a few lectures on astronomy and a look through a telescope their neat little universe begins to fall apart. The sheer hugeness of the heavenly bodies and the immensity of space overwhelm them. The earth is but a microscopic speck in the vastness of space, a man but an infinitesimal pinpoint on the earth's surface, and God somewhere out beyond the farthest star, billions of light years removed—how then could God become man and dwell among us? And of what account is a man, insignificantly small and pathetically short-lived?

To think in this way is to confuse size with quality; it is to think ignobly of the Most High God; it is to identify Him with matter and make Him a servant of time and space; it is to degrade our concept of Deity and to fall victim to unbelief.

The truth is that one soul made in the image of God is more precious to Him than all the starry universe. Astronomy deals with space and matter and motion; theology deals with life and personality and the mystery of being. The body of the psalmist David, for instance, though of average size, was so small that it might have been tucked away in a crevice among the mountains of Judaea and never found, though men had searched for a thousand years. That is size, and it is not very important. But in some inspired hour David wrote the Shepherd Psalm! That is quality, and how precious it is may be inferred from the sound of ten thousand voices singing that psalm every Sunday of the year around the whole world.

The Church is dedicated to things that matter. Quality matters. Let's not be led astray by the size of things.

Chapter 18

Let's Be Humble About Our Orthodoxy

CHRISTIANITY IS rarely found pure. Apart from Christ and His inspired apostles probably no believer or company of believers in the history of the world has ever held the truth in total purity.

One great saint believed that the truth is so vast and mighty that no one is capable of taking it all in, and that it requires the whole company of ransomed souls properly to reflect the whole body of revealed truth.

The light has shone upon men and nations, and (God be praised) it has shone with sufficient clarity to enable millions to travel home in its glow; but no believer, however pure his heart or however obedient his life, has ever been able to receive it as it shines from the Throne unmodified by his own mental stuff. As a lump of clay when grasped by the human hand remains clay but cannot escape the imprint of the hand, so the truth of God when grasped by the human mind remains truth but bears upon it the image of the mind that grasps it. Truth cannot enter a passive mind. It must be received into the mind by an active mental response, and the act of receiving it tends to alter it to a greater or less degree.

As the sun's rays are bent when passing through a prism, so has the light of God been bent when passing through the hearts of men. Sin, temperament, prejudice, early education, cultural influences, prevailing vogues: all have worked to throw the eyes of the heart out of focus and distort the inward vision.

Of course I refer here to theological and religious truth. How pure this truth is in any place at any given time is revealed by the moral standards of those who hold the truth and by religious practices among the churches generally. Spiritual truth (by which I mean the disclosures of the Holy Spirit to the human spirit) is always the same. The Spirit always says the same thing to whomsoever He speaks and altogether without regard to passing doctrinal emphases or theological vogues. He flashes the beauty of Christ upon the wondering heart, and the awed spirit receives it with a minimum of interference. Wesley and Watts were worlds apart in their theology, but they could and did love and sing the same hymns of pure worship and adoration. The Spirit united them to worship even though their respective views of truth separated them doctrinally.

Each age has interpreted Christianity after its own fashion. The religion of the barnstorming American revivalists of the nineteenth century was certainly something different from that of Luther or the medieval mystics or the apostolic fathers. The bishops who met at Nicea in the fourth century to defend the faith of Christ from the attack of the Arians surely differed radically from the scholars and saints who stood to defend that same faith from the attack of the higher critics in the early twentieth century.

Theology has a tendency to run to modes just as does philosophy. The Christian teachers of the Middle Ages bore down hard upon the vanity of life and the innate wickedness of the body. In the early days of America the prevailing doctrine was hell, and the popular preachers of those times revealed more details about that terrible place than were known to the inspired writers of the Scriptures. In more recent times it was discovered again that God is love, and the love of God for mankind became the chief theme of sermon and song throughout the evangelical world.

Right now we are in another period of transition, and blessed is the man that knows where we are going. Whatever direction the theological wind may set there are two things of which we may be certain: One is that God will not leave Himself without a witness. There will always be some who hold the creed of Christ, the inspired outline of Christian doctrine. Saving truth will never be completely hidden from the sight of men. The poor in spirit, the penitent, will always find Christ close at hand ready to save them. The other is that the Holy Spirit is the true conservator of orthodoxy and will invariably say the same thing to meek and trusting souls. Illuminated hearts are sure to agree at the point where the light falls.

Our only real danger is that we may grieve the blessed Spirit into silence and so be left to the mercy of our intellects. Then we shall have Christian scholars in abundance but we'll be short on adoring saints. We'll have defenders of the faith who can overawe their opponents with their logic and their learning, but we'll be without prophets and mystics and hymnists. We'll have the bush, pruned and trimmed and properly cultivated, but in the bush there will be no fire.

Truth is forever the same, but modes and emphases and interpretations vary. It is a cheering thought that Christ can adapt Himself to any race or age or people. He will give life and light to any man or woman anywhere in the world regardless of doctrinal emphasis or prevailing religious customs, provided that man or woman takes Him as He is and trusts Him without reservation. The Spirit never bears witness to an argument about Christ, but He never fails to witness to a proclamation of Christ crucified, dead and buried, and now ascended to the right hand of the Majesty on high.

The conclusion of the matter is that we should not assume that we have all the truth and that we are mistaken in nothing. Rather we should kneel in adoration before the pierced feet of Him who is the Truth and honor Him by humble obedience to His words.

Chapter 19

Refined or Removed?

WE CHRISTIANS must look sharp that our Christianity does not simply refine our sins without removing them.

The work of Christ as Saviour is twofold: to "save his people from their sins" and to reunite them forever with the God from whom sin had alienated them.

God's holy character requires that He refuse to admit sin into His fellowship. Through the redemption which is in Christ Jesus mercy may pardon the returning sinner and place him judicially beyond the reach of the broken law; but not the boundless grace nor the infinite kindness of God can make it morally congruous for a pure being to have communion with an impure one. It is necessary to the moral health of the universe that God divide the light from the darkness and that He say at last to every sinner, "Depart from me, ye that work iniquity."

This certainly is no new thought. Christian theologians have all recognized the necessity for an adequate purgation of the inner springs of moral conduct and the impartation of a renewed nature to the believer before he is ready for the fellowship of God. Our hymnists also have seen and wrestled with this great problem—and thanks be to God, have found the answer, too.

Binney felt the weight of this problem and stated it along with the solution in a little known but deeply spiritual hymn:

> Eternal Light! eternal Light!
>> How pure that soul must be
> When placed within Thy searching sight,
>> It shrinks not, but with calm delight
> Can live, and look on Thee.
>
> O how shall I, whose native sphere
>> Is dark, whose mind is dim,
> Before the Ineffable appear,
> And on my naked spirit bear
>> That uncreated beam?
>
> There is a way for man to rise
>> To that sublime abode:
> An offering and a sacrifice,
> A Holy Spirit's energies,
>> An Advocate with God.

The offering and the sacrifice and the sanctifying energies of the Holy Spirit are indeed sufficient to prepare the soul for communion with God. This the Bible declares and this ten thousand times ten thousand witnesses confirm. The big danger is that we assume that we have been delivered from our sins when we have in reality only exchanged one kind of sin for another. This is the peril that lies in wait for everyone. It need not discourage us nor turn us back, but it should make us watchful.

We must, for instance, be careful that our repentance is not simply a change of location. Whereas we once sinned in the far country among the swineherds, we are now chumming with religious persons, considerably cleaner and much more respectable in appearance, to be sure, but no nearer to true heart purity than we were before.

Again, pride may by religious influence be refined to a quiet self-esteem, skillfully dissembled by a neat use of Bible words that meant everything to those who first used them but which may only serve to disguise a deep self-love which is to God a hateful and intolerable thing. The real trouble is thus not cleared up, but only driven underground.

The gossip and troublemaker sometimes at conversion turns into a "spiritual counselor," but often a closer look will reveal the same restless, inquisitive spirit at work that made her a nuisance before her conversion. The whole thing has been refined and given a religious appearance, but actually nothing radical has happened. She is still running the same stand, only on the other side of the street. There has been a certain refinement of the sin, but definitely not a removal of it. This is Satan's most successful way of getting into the church to cause weakness, backsliding and division.

Many a business transaction which among worldly men we would brand as sharp practice, when carried on by a Christian after he has prayed over it is hailed as a remarkable answer to prayer and a proof that God is a "partner" in the affair.

These are illustrations only, intended to show how sin may alter its appearance without changing its nature, and are not to be taken to mean that I am opposed to Christian counselors or businessmen who pray over their affairs. The contrary is true. That church is blessed indeed which has in it a few persons with the gift of discernment to whom weak and troubled Christians may come for help in times of crisis. And blessed is the businessman today who has learned to pray his way through red tape and taxes. Without the help of God I do not see how businessmen stay sane in this frightful rat race we call civilization.

The temptation to spare the best of the sheep and the cattle is very strong in all of us. Like Saul before us we are willing enough to slay the scrubby sheep and the old sway-back steers, but Adam and the devil join to try to persuade us to keep the fattest beasts alive. And many of us fall for the old trick. We make pets of the cattle we should have destroyed and their bleatings and bellowings are heard throughout all Christendom.

The will of God is that sin should be removed, not merely refined. Let's walk in His will.

Chapter 20

Are We Losing
Our "Oh!"?

WE WHO SPEAK the English language have in that language a most remarkable instrument for the communication of ideas.

Emerson said of Shakespeare that he more than any other man had the ability to say anything he wanted to say; any idea his mind could entertain, his mouth could utter. What Emerson did not remember to say (if my memory serves me) was that Shakespeare's genius was indebted greatly to the fluidity and fullness of the English tongue. Without such a free and abundant vocabulary as English affords, even the mighty Bard of Avon could not have risen so high nor soared so far. However great his mind, he required a language capable of receiving and expressing what his mind conceived. And that he had in his beloved English.

Webster's Unabridged Dictionary lists 550,000 words. And it is a solemn and beautiful thought that in our worship of God there sometimes rush up from the depths of our souls feelings that all this wealth of words is not sufficient to express. To be articulate at certain times we are compelled to fall back upon "Oh!" or "O!"—a primitive exclamatory sound that is hardly a word at all and that scarcely admits of a definition.

Vocabularies are formed by many minds over long periods and are capable of expressing whatever the mind is capable of entertaining. But when the heart, on its knees, moves into the awesome Presence and hears with fear and wonder things not lawful to utter, then the mind falls flat, and words, previously its faithful servants, become weak and totally incapable of telling what the heart hears and sees. In that awful moment the worshiper can only cry "Oh!" And that simple exclamation becomes more eloquent than learned speech and, I have no doubt, is dearer to God than any oratory.

It is not by accident that the idiom of the Christian religion abounds with exclamations. Christianity contemplates things transcendent and seeks to engage the infinite and the absolute. It approaches the Holy of Holies and looks with astonished wonder upon the face of God; then language, no matter how full or how facile, is simply not adequate. "O the depths of the riches both of the wisdom and knowledge of God! how unsearchable are his judgments, and his ways past finding out" (Rom. 11:33). The exclamation "O" could not be omitted from that rhapsody. It is the fountain out of which everything else flows.

Many of our Christian hymns reveal this same exclamatory quality, chiefly because they embody an intensity of feeling that rises above rational meanings and definitions into the realm of the numinous. The Moravian Hymnal, for instance, lists about three hundred verse lines that begin with "O." While it would not be wise to press this too far (since literary custom may dictate the use of emotional language where no particular emotion is present) still the fact that there is such a large number of exclamations among the hymns surely does have real meaning for us.

In the inspired Scriptures, where no imperfection is to be found, the exclamatory vocable occurs constantly. Prophets and psalmists continually find themselves on the brink of the infinite gazing into an abysm of divinity that quite overwhelms them and squeezes from their hearts such bursts of feeling as mere words cannot express. It is then that "Oh!" and "Ah!" come spontaneously to their lips, as when Jeremiah, upon hearing the voice of the Lord, responds, "Ah, Lord God! behold, I cannot speak: for I am a child"; or when Ezekiel standing in the valley of bones cries out, "O Lord God, thou knowest."

In theology there is no "Oh!" and this is a significant if not an ominous thing. Theology seeks to reduce what may be known of God to intellectual terms, and as long as the intellect can comprehend it can find words to express itself. When God Himself appears before the mind, awesome, vast and incomprehensible, then the mind sinks into silence and the heart cries out "O Lord God!" There is the difference between theological knowledge and spiritual experience, the difference between knowing God by hearsay and knowing Him by acquaintance. And the difference is not verbal merely; it is real and serious and vital.

We Christians should watch lest we lose the "Oh!" from our hearts. There is real danger these days that we shall fall victim to the prophets of poise and the purveyors of tranquility, and our Christianity be reduced to a mere evangelical humanism that is never disturbed about anything nor overcome by any "trances of thought and mountings of the mind." When we become too glib in prayer we are most surely talking to ourselves. When the calm listing of requests and the courteous giving of proper thanks take the place of the burdened prayer that finds utterance difficult we should beware the next step, for our direction is surely down whether we know it or not.

Churches and missionary societies should keep always before them the knowledge that progress can be made only by the "Ohs" and "Ahs" of Spirit-filled hearts. These are the pain cries of the fruitful mother about to give birth. For them there is no substitute; not plans nor programs nor techniques can avail without them. They indicate the presence of the Holy Spirit making intercessions with groanings that cannot be uttered. And this is God's only method in the local church or on the mission field.

Chapter 21

Only a Few Things Matter

IT HAS BEEN suggested here before that life, for all its apparent complexities, is at bottom very simple indeed if we could only realize it. Thank God, only a few things matter. The rest are incidental and unimportant.

Nothing that matters is new. "There is no new thing under the sun," said Solomon, and he could hardly have meant that there had been no mechanical development or social or political changes under the sun, for he observed elsewhere that man has "sought out many inventions," and he had himself instituted quite a number of changes in the royal routine. The city of Jerusalem he left behind him when he died was quite another city from the one he took over from his father David. External changes were numerous even in those days, but in nature and in man nothing was new; and it was of these that Solomon wrote.

Nothing is new that matters and nothing that matters can be modernized. One way to evaluate anything in the world around us is to check for possible modernization. If it can be modernized you may safely put it far down in the scale of human values. Only the unchanged and the unchanging should be accounted worthy of lasting consideration by beings made in the image of God.

Should some reader impatiently brush me off as hopelessly old-fashioned I shall not be offended. To escape the illusion of the temporal requires a free mind and a heart deeply engrossed in eternal thoughts and filled with immortal yearnings. And present-day Christianity simply does not produce that kind of mentality. Neither can we hope with Wordsworth "that mellower years will bring a riper mind and clearer insight," for our direction is away from this and not toward it. Unless we have been enlightened deep in the Spirit of truth, the passing of time will not help us. Rather it may confirm us in our carnality. There is such a thing as spiritual senility. It is the natural result of failure over a prolonged period to live in the light of revealed truth; and any of us can slide into it unless we walk humbly and circumspectly.

Almost everything that men value today has been developed from some primitive archetype: the stream-lined auto from the wheel, the skyscraper from the stone arch, the supersonic airplane from the kite, our highly complex monetary system from the cowrie shell or its equivalent, our extremely efficient methods of communication from hieroglyphics or the jungle drum. I think it would be possible to trace about 98 per cent of the items that compose our modern civilized world back to their primitive originals. Yet I reassert with emphasis that nothing new matters and nothing that really matters can be modernized.

What really matters after all? My personal relation to God matters. That takes priority over everything else. A man may be born in a sanitary hospital, receive his education in progressive schools, ride in an air-conditioned car, sleep on a foam rubber mattress, wear synthetic clothing, eat vitamin-enriched food, read by fluorescent lights, speak across 12,000 miles of empty space to a friend on the other side of the world, lose his anxieties by taking tranquilizing pills, die without pain by the aid of some new drug and be laid to rest in a memorial park as lovely as a country garden; yet what will all this profit him if he must later rise to face in judgment a God who knows him not and whom he does not know? To come at last before the bar of eternal justice with no one to plead his cause and to be banished forever from the presence of the great Judge—is that man any better off than if he had died a naked savage in the hinterlands of Borneo?

No man can afford to live or die under the frowning displeasure of God. Yet, name one modern device that can save him from it. Where can a man find security? Can philosophy help him? or psychology? or science? or "progress"? or atoms or wonder drugs or vitamins? No. Only Christ can help him, and His aid is as old as man's sin and man's need. The naked aborigine is as near to God (and as far from Him) as the Ph.D. Nothing new can save my soul; neither can saving grace be modernized. We must each come as Abel came, by atoning blood and faith demonstrated in repentance. No new way has been discovered. The old way is the true way and there is no new way. The Lamb of God was slain "before the foundation of the world."

A few other things matter to be sure, but they begin there, go out from there and return there again. They are that we trust Christ completely, carry our cross daily, love God and our fellow men, walk in the light as God gives us to understand it; that we love mercy, and walk uprightly; that we fulfill our commission as ambassadors of Christ among men; that we grow in grace and in the knowledge of God and come at last to our end like a ripe shock of corn at harvest time.

These are the things that matter. These things are always critical, yet few recognize them as being so. It is all but impossible these days to get attention to the things that matter. Only as the servants of God veer away from these serious and eternal things to talk of politics or world events or sports or science will the nervous and distraught victims of time and space give them a hearing. Yet these eternal truths are all the Bible teaches and all we are authorized to proclaim.

Chapter 22

The Value of a
Sanctified Imagination

LIKE EVERY OTHER power belonging to us, the imagination may be either a blessing or a curse, depending altogether upon how it is used and how well it is disciplined.

We all have to some degree the power to imagine. This gift enables us to see meanings in material objects, to observe similarities between things which at first appear wholly unlike each other. It permits us to know that which the senses can never tell us, for by it we are able to see through sense impressions to the reality that lies behind things.

Every advance made by mankind in any field began as an idea to which nothing for the time corresponded. The mind of the inventor simply took bits of familiar ideas and made out of them something which was not only wholly unfamiliar but which up to that time was altogether nonexistent. Thus we "create" things and by so doing prove ourselves to have been made in the image of the Creator. That fallen man has often used his creative powers in the service of evil does not invalidate our argument. Any talent may be used for evil as well as for good, but every talent comes from God nevertheless.

That the imagination is of great value in the service of God may be denied by some persons who have erroneously confused the word "imaginative" with the word "imaginary."

The gospel of Jesus Christ has no truck with things imaginary. The most realistic book in the world is the Bible. God is real, men are real and so is sin and so are death and hell, toward which sin inevitably leads. The presence of God is not imaginary, neither is prayer the indulgence of a delightful fancy. The objects that engage the praying man's attention, while not material, are nevertheless completely real; more certainly real, it will at last be admitted, than any earthly object.

The value of the cleansed imagination in the sphere of religion lies in its power to perceive in natural things shadows of things spiritual. It enables the reverent man to

> "See the world in a grain of sand
> And eternity in an hour."

The weakness of the Pharisee in days of old was his lack of imagination, or what amounted to the same thing, his refusal to let it enter the field of religion. He saw the text with its carefully guarded theological definition and he saw nothing beyond.

> "A primrose by the river's brim
> A yellow primrose was to him,
> And it was nothing more."

When Christ came with His blazing spiritual penetration and His fine moral sensitivity He appeared to the Pharisee to be a devotee of another kind of religion, which indeed He was if the world had only understood. He could see the soul of the text while the Pharisee could see only the body, and he could always prove Christ wrong by an appeal to the letter of the law or to an interpretation hallowed by tradition. The breach between them was too great to permit them to coexist; so the Pharisee, who was in a position to do it, had the young Seer put to death. So it has always been, and so I suppose it will always be till the earth is filled with the knowledge of the Lord as the waters cover the sea.

The imagination, since it is a faculty of the natural mind, must necessarily suffer both from its intrinsic limitations and from an inherent bent toward evil. While the word as found in the King James Bible usually means not imagination at all, but merely the reasonings of sinful men, I yet do not write to excuse the unsanctified imagination. I well know that from such have flowed as from a polluted fountain streams of evil ideas which have throughout the years led to lawless and destructive conduct on the part of men.

A purified and Spirit-controlled imagination is, however, quite another thing, and it is this I have in mind here. I long to see the imagination released from its prison and given to its proper place among the sons of the new creation. What I am trying to describe here is the sacred gift of seeing, the ability to peer beyond the veil and gaze with astonished wonder upon the beauties and mysteries of things holy and eternal.

The stodgy pedestrian mind does no credit to Christianity. Let it dominate the church long enough and it will force her to take one of two directions: either toward liberalism, where she will find relief in a false freedom, or toward the world, where she will find an enjoyable but fatal pleasure.

But I wonder whether this is not all included in the words of our Lord as recorded in the Gospel of John: "Howbeit when he, the Spirit of truth, is come, he will guide you into all truth: for he shall not speak of himself; but whatsoever he shall hear, that shall he speak: and he will shew you things to come. He shall glorify me: for he shall receive of mine, and shall shew it unto you" (16:13, 14).

To possess a Spirit-indwelt mind is the Christian's privilege under grace, and this embraces all I have been trying to say here.

Chapter 23

Let's Go Off the Defensive

IN THE KINGDOM of God the surest way to lose something is to try to protect it, and the best way to keep it is to let it go.

The law of keeping by surrendering and losing by defending is revealed by our Lord in His celebrated but little understood declaration: "If any man will come after me, let him deny himself, and take up his cross, and follow me" (Matt. 16:24).

Here is seen the glaring disparity between the ways of God and the ways of men. When the world takes its hands off a prized possession someone grabs it and disappears. Therefore the world must conserve by defending. So men hoard their heart's treasures, lock up their possessions, protect their good name with libel laws, hedge themselves about with protective devices of every sort and guard their shores with powerful armed forces. This is all according to Adam's philosophy which springs from his fallen nature and is confirmed by thousands of years of practical experience. To challenge it is to invite the scorn of mankind; and yet our Lord did challenge it.

To be specific, Christ did not condemn the world for defending its own; He turned from the fallen world and spoke about another world altogether, a world where Adam's philosophy is invalid and where his techniques are inoperative. He spoke of the kingdom of God whose laws are exactly opposite to those of the kingdom of man.

Long before Christ laid down the spiritual principles that should govern the new kingdom God had said by the mouth of His prophet, "My thoughts are not your thoughts, neither are your ways my ways" (Isa. 55:8); and Christ said elsewhere, "That which is highly esteemed among men is abomination in the sight of God" (Luke 16:15). Between spiritual laws and the laws of human society there is a great gulf. In His wisdom God moves on the high road according to His eternal purposes; man on the low road moves along as best he can, improvising and muddling through according to no certain plan, hoping that things will come out all right and almost always seeing his hopes disappointed.

The true Christian is a child of two worlds. He lives among fallen men, receives all of his earlier concepts from them and develops a fallen view of life along with everyone from Adam on. When he is regenerated and inducted into the new creation he is called to live according to the laws and principles that underlie the new kingdom, but all his training and his thinking have been according to the old. So he may, unless he is very wise and prayerful, find himself trying to live a heavenly life after an earthly pattern. This is what Paul called "carnal" living. The issues of the new Christian life are influenced by the automatic responses of the old life and confusion results.

Against this background it is easy to understand why so many Christians instinctively cling to their treasures, defend their possessions and fight for their reputation. They are reacting after the old pattern which they had followed so naturally and so long.

It takes real faith to begin to live the life of heaven while still upon the earth, for this requires that we rise above the law of moral gravitation and bring to our everyday living the high wisdom of God. And since this wisdom is contrary to that of the world, conflict is bound to result. This, however, is a small price to pay for the inestimable privilege of following Christ.

It is vitally important that we move up into the Spirit and cease to defend ourselves. I have never met a victorious Christian who was on the defensive, but I have met I cannot tell how many jumpy, skittish and thoroughly unhappy Christians who were burning up their energies in a vain endeavor to protect themselves. These poor, dejected souls imagine that someone is forever trying, as they say, to "put something over" on them. The result is worry, resentfulness and a kind of low-pressure hostility toward everyone they may have reason to believe is after something they possess.

My earnest advice to all such nervous souls is to turn everything over to God and relax. A real Christian need not defend his possession nor his position. God will take care of both. Let go of your treasures and the Lord will keep them for you unto life eternal. Hang unto them and they will bring you nothing but trouble and misery to the end of your days.

It is better to throw our little all to the four winds than to get old and sour defending it. It is better to be cheated a few times than to develop a constant suspicion that someone is trying to cheat us. It is better to have the house burglarized than to spend the rest of our days and nights sitting with a rifle across our knees watching over it. Give it up, and keep it. Defend it, and lose it. That is a law of the kingdom and it applies to every regenerated soul. We can afford to trust God; but we can't afford not to.

Chapter 24

The Tragedy of Wasted Religious Activity

THERE IS PROBABLY not another field of human activity where there is so much waste as in the field of religion.

It is altogether possible to waste an hour in church or even in a prayer meeting. The popular "attend the church of your choice" signs that have lately been appearing everywhere may have some small value if they do no more than remind a materialistic civilization that this world is not all and that there are some treasures that cannot be bought with money. Yet we must not forget that a man may attend church for a lifetime and be none the better for it.

In the average church we hear the same prayers repeated each Sunday year in and year out with, one would suspect, not the remotest expectation that they will be answered. It is enough, it seems, that they have been uttered. The familiar phrase, the religious tone, the emotionally loaded words have their superficial and temporary effect, but the worshiper is no nearer to God, no better morally and no surer of heaven than he was before. Yet every Sunday morning for twenty years he goes through the same routine and, allowing two hours for him to leave his house, sit through a church service and return to his house again, he has wasted more than 170 twelve-hour days with this exercise in futility.

The writer to the Hebrews says that some professed Christians were marking time and getting nowhere. They had had plenty of opportunity to grow, but they had not grown; they had had sufficient time to mature, yet they were still babes; so he exhorted them to leave their meaningless religious round and press on to perfection (Heb. 5:11-6:3).

It is possible to have motion without progress, and this describes much of the activity among Christians today. It is simply lost motion.

In God there is motion, but never wasted motion; He always works toward a predetermined end. Being made in His image, we are by nature constituted so that we are justifying our existence only when we are working with a purpose in mind. Aimless activity is beneath the worth and dignity of a human being. Activity that does not result in progress toward a goal is wasted; yet most Christians have no clear end toward which they are striving. On the endless religious merry-go-round they continue to waste time and energy, of which, God knows, they never had much and have less each hour. This is a tragedy worthy of the mind of an Aeschylus or a Dante.

Back of this tragic waste there is usually one of three causes: The Christian is either ignorant of the Scriptures, unbelieving or disobedient.

I think most Christians are simply uninstructed. They may have been talked into the kingdom when they were only half ready. Any convert made within the last thirty years was almost certainly told that he had but to take Jesus as his personal Saviour and all would be well. Possibly some counselor may have added that he now had eternal life and would most surely go to heaven when he died, if indeed the Lord does not return and carry him away in triumph before the unpleasant moment of death arrives.

After that first hurried entrance into the kingdom there is usually not much more said. The new convert finds himself with a hammer and a saw and no blueprint. He has not the remotest notion what he is supposed to build, so he settles down to the dull routine of polishing his tools once each Sunday and putting them back in their box.

Sometimes, however, the Christian wastes his efforts because of unbelief. Possibly we are all guilty of this to some degree. In our private prayers and in our public services we are forever asking God to do things that He either has already done or cannot do because of our unbelief. We plead for Him to speak when He has already spoken and is at that very moment speaking. We ask Him to come when He is already present and waiting for us to recognize Him. We beg the Holy Spirit to fill us while all the time we are preventing Him by our doubts.

Of course the Christian can hope for no manifestation of God while he lives in a state of disobedience. Let a man refuse to obey God on some clear point, let

him set his will stubbornly to resist any command-
ment of Christ, and the rest of his religious activities
will be wasted. He may go to church for fifty years
to no profit. He may tithe, teach, preach, sing, write
or edit or run a Bible conference till he gets too old to
navigate and have nothing but ashes at the last. "To
obey is better than sacrifice."

I need only add that all this tragic waste is unnecessary. The believing Christian will relish every moment in church and will profit by it. The instructed,
obedient Christian will yield to God as the clay to the
potter, and the result will be not waste but glory
everlasting.

Chapter 25

The Transmutation
of Wealth

THE BIBLE HAS a great deal to say about wealth. Our
Lord dealt with the matter forthrightly, as did also
Paul and others of the New Testament writers. What
they said is on record and is deserving of a more careful study than most Christians give it.

Wealth, of course, may exist in many forms and
on a number of levels. A thing may be valuable in
itself, or it may be intrinsically worthless but have
an arbitrary value attached to it and so become a
much sought after treasure among men. It would,
for instance, be difficult to conceive of anything less
valuable in itself than a cowrie shell, yet by common
consent that worthless shell is made to stand for sweet
potatoes or pigs, things having actual value for the
people who must subsist upon them. And surely
no one imagines that a bank note, a money order
or a check has any worth apart from that attributed
to it by law or custom.

One form of wealth for which little excuse can be
found consists of trinkets to which a wholly artificial

value has been attached, such as antiques, autographs and first editions. These constitute wealth in the minds of only a relatively few persons, but because most of these are the blasé rich, surfeited with too much of everything, these quaint playthings often sell for fabulous prices.

Another form of wealth consists of those humble items necessary to human life on earth—grain, oil, vegetables, fruit, wool, water, lumber; and these are not to be despised even by the most heavenly-minded person. They are gifts from God and are to be received with meekness and thanksgiving.

Other finer treasures are those that pertain to our physical constitution, such as health, sight, hearing; treasures of the mind, as freedom, friendship, love, tranquillity; aesthetic treasures, such as music, literature and all things good and beautiful.

Above all these and incomparably greater than any or all of them are those treasures eternal in the heavens of which Christ spoke in His sermon on the mount and which the apostle Peter described as an inheritance incorruptible and undefiled and that fadeth not away. These become more real to us as we move on into conscious union with God, and the lower forms of wealth lose their value correspondingly.

Our Lord identified the highest form of wealth as "the kingdom of God, and his righteousness." This embraces about all the redeemed man can desire through all eternal years. Yet there was not in the teachings of Christ any trace of that voluntary pauperism that held earthly goods to be evil. This de-

veloped later among the Christian monks and ancho-
rites. It arose from a misunderstanding of our Lord's
words or was borrowed from Buddhism. Christ frankly recognized the value of meat and drink and clothing. He called them "all these things," assured His
followers that the Father knew they needed them,
and promised that He would give them as a bonus
to those who sought the higher wealth first (Matt.
6:25-33).

Knowing the tendency of the human heart to become unduly attached to earthly goods, Christ warned
against it. The "things" which the Father gives are
to be understood as provisional merely and must never
be considered our real treasure. The heart always
returns to its real treasure, and if a man holds corn to
be a real form of wealth his heart will be where his
corn is. Many a man has his heart locked up in a
bank vault, and many a woman has her heart in her
jewel box or stored at the furrier's. It is a great moral
tragedy when anything as wonderful as the human
heart comes to rest on the earth and fails to rise to its
own proper place in God and in heaven.

Treasure, incidentally, may be discovered by this
fourfold test: (1) It is what we value most. (2) It
is what we would hate most to lose. (3) It is what
our thoughts turn to most frequently when we are
free to think of what we will. (4) It is what affords
us the greatest pleasure.

One of the glories of the Christian religion is that
faith and love can transmute lower values into higher

ones. Earthly possessions can be turned into heavenly treasures.

It is like this: A twenty-dollar bill, useless in itself, can be transmuted into milk and eggs and fruit to feed hungry children. Physical and mental powers, valuable in themselves, can be transmuted into still higher values, such as a home and an education for a growing family. Human speech, a very gift of God to mankind, can become consolation for the bereaved or hope for the disconsolate, and it can rise higher and break into prayer and praise to the Most High God.

As base a thing as money often is, it yet can be transmuted into everlasting treasure. It can be converted into food for the hungry and clothing for the poor; it can keep a missionary actively winning lost men to the light of the gospel and thus transmute itself into heavenly values.

Any temporal possession can be turned into everlasting wealth. Whatever is given to Christ is immediately touched with immortality. Hosanna to God in the highest!

Chapter 26

The Christian Is Wiser
Than He Thinks

IT IS IRONIC that this generation which more than any other in history preaches the brotherhood of man is also the generation most torn by unbrotherly strife.

War, either cold or hot, has plagued the earth incessantly from the day Cain slew Abel to the present moment; but never before in the history of the race have there been such deep hatreds, such alienation of hearts, such suspicion, such bitter accusations, such threats, such phrenetic competition to perfect and pile up horror weapons capable of wiping out whole cities instantaneously.

For the first time in human history the language of generals and statesmen is beginning to sound like the Apocalypse, and the frightening thing is that science has given the war lords the power to bring apocalyptic destruction upon the world.

Science, the sweet talking goddess which but a short time ago smilingly disposed of the Bible as a trustworthy guide and took the world by the hand to lead it into a man-made millennium, has turned out to be a dragon capable of destroying that same world with a flick of her fiery tail.

The world talks of peace, and by peace it means the absence of war. What it overlooks is that there is another meaning of the word, namely, tranquillity of heart, and without that kind of peace the peace of the world will continue to be but an unattainable dream. As long as peace between nations continues to depend upon the shifting moods of choleric old men filled with hatred and frustration at their approaching dissolution, and who are ready to pull the world down with them into the bottomless pit, just that long will there be no peace among nations.

In spite of all the books lately published, inward tranquillity cannot be found on the earth. Peace has fled the halls of learning and if found at all is found now among the lowly. Once men sought philosophy as a way of life; from her they learned to be satisfied with their lot, resigned and patient with men and with nature. Socrates, Marcus Aurelius, Epictetus—these could teach Khrushchev, Nasser and Tito, but from such as these such as they will not learn. Hate, greed, megalomania and the mad ambition that in every generation "o'erleaps itself" drive the leaders of nations savagely to kill and destroy for the furtherance of their incredibly wicked ends.

But we need not look at kings and generals to discover the bankruptcy of the world. Go but to the corner store; drive your car down a busy street; take a quick glance at the crowds getting on or off a bus; try to buy a house or to sell one; in short, engage in any common pursuit and the secret is immediately out. Among the sons of fallen men there is no peace of mind or of heart.

True peace is a gift of God and today it is found only in the minds of innocent children and in the hearts of trustful Christians. "Peace I leave with you," said our Lord at the close of His earthly ministry; "my peace I give unto you: not as the world giveth, give I unto you. Let not your heart be troubled, neither let it be afraid."

It is time that we Christians awake to the fact that the world cannot help us in anything that matters. Not the educators nor the legislators nor the scientists can bring us tranquillity of heart, and without tranquillity whatever else they give us is useless at last. For more than half a lifetime I have listened to their promises, and they have so far failed to make good on one of them. To turn to God is now the only reasonable thing to do; we have no second choice. "Lord, to whom shall we go? thou hast the words of eternal life."

It is an ironic thought too that fallen men, though they cannot fulfill their promises, are always able to make good on their threats. For decades they have been promising us a warless world where peace and brotherhood shall sit quiet as a brooding dove. All they have given us is the control of a few diseases and the debilitating comforts of push-button living. These have extended our lives a little longer so we are now able to stay around to see our generation die one by

110

one; and when the riper years come upon us they retire us by compulsion and turn us out to clutter up a world that has no place for us, a world that does not understand us and that we do not understand.

But A-bombs and H-bombs and intercontinental missiles and atomic submarines able to belch irradiant death upon us from below the surface of the sea— these they have perfected and stand ready to use any time the undisciplined temper of some president or prime minister gets sufficiently out of hand.

In view of all this how wise is the man who has made the God of Jacob his hope and has taken refuge in the Rock of Ages. He has repudiated a world that can make good only on its threats and has fled for refuge to the Saviour who waits long before carrying out His threats but is ready any moment to fulfill a promise.

Maybe the great of the world have underestimated the Christian after all. When the big day comes he may stand like Abraham above the burning plain and watch the smoke rising from the cities that forgot God. Neither science nor learning can quench the fires of judgment in that day, but a Christian can steal a quick look at Calvary and know that his judgment is past.

Chapter 27

The Fellowship
of the Brethren

ONE THING THAT instantly strikes the intelligent reader
of the New Testament is the communal nature of the
Christian faith. The social pronouns—we, they, us,
them—are found everywhere. God's ideal is a fellowship of faith, a Christian community. He never intended that salvation should be received and enjoyed
by the individual apart from the larger company of
believers.

It is true that for each one there must be a personal
encounter with God, and often that encounter takes
place in the loneliness and silence of retirement. In
that sacred moment there must be only God and the
individual soul. The mysterious operation of God in
regenerating grace and His further work of the Spirit's
anointing are transactions so highly personal that no
third party can know or understand what is taking
place.

There are other experiences deep and wholly inward that cannot be shared with any other: Jacob at
Bethel and Peniel, Moses at the burning bush, Christ

in the garden, John in the Isle of Patmos are Bible examples, and Christian biography will reveal many more. A community of believers must be composed of persons who have each one met God in individual experience. No matter how large the family, each child must be born individually. Even twins or triplets are born one at a time. So it is in the local church. Each member must be born of the Spirit individually.

It will not escape the discerning reader that while each child is born separate from the rest it is born into a family, and after that must live in the fellowship of the rest of the household. And the man who comes to Christ in the loneliness of personal repentance and faith is also born into a family. The church is called the household of God, and it is the ideal place to rear young Christians. Just as a child will not grow up to be a normal adult if forced to live alone, so the Christian who withdraws from the fellowship of other Christians will suffer great soul injury as a result. Such a one can never hope to develop normally. He'll get too much of himself and not enough of other people; and that is not good.

God has so created us that we need each other. We may and should go into our closet and pray to our heavenly Father in secret, but when the prayer is ended we should go back to our people. That is where we belong.

To live within the religious family does not mean that we must approve everything that is done there. The prophets of Israel were often compelled to rebuke and warn their people, but they never left the bosom of Judaism. Even Christ went each Sabbath day and worshiped with the rest. The reformers and revivalists of post-Biblical times invariably lived close to the people. The loneliest and severest of them had their company of like-minded souls in which they found the help and consolation their grieving hearts required. Their example does not have the authority of revealed truth, but it does provide a rule we do well to follow.

No one is wise enough to live alone, nor good enough nor strong enough. God has made us to a large degree dependent upon each other. From our brethren we can learn how to do things and sometimes also we can learn how not to do them. The best of singers must have a coach if he would avoid having his faults become chronic. The preacher who hears only himself preach will soon accept even his worst idiosyncrasies as marks of excellence. We need to listen to others that we may learn what to correct in ourselves. This is true also of things moral and spiritual within the Christian family circle. A weak and faulty Christian, without his knowing it, can turn us from his way of life, and every holy and fruitful saint within our circle of fellowship becomes a goad to spur us onward toward a more perfect life.

Next to God Himself we need each other most. We are His sheep and it is our nature to live with the flock. And too, it might be well to remember that should we for a moment lose sight of the Shepherd we only have to go where His flock is to find Him again. The Shepherd always stays with His flock.

Chapter 28

The Unity of All Things

THOUGHT AND PRAYER and a spiritual understanding of the Scriptures will reveal the unity of all things.

What appear to be a million separate and unrelated phenomena are actually but different phases of a single whole. Everything is related to everything else.

It cannot be otherwise, seeing that God is one. All His words and acts are related to each other by being related to Him. He revealed Himself in history as the world's Redeemer, "here a little, there a little" as fallen men were able to receive it, and everything He made known concerning Himself agreed with itself and with all else that had been previously revealed.

In God there is no *was* or *will be*, but a continuous and unbroken *is*. In Him history and prophecy are one and the same. To us men, submerged in time, it may properly be said that prophecy is history foretold and history is prophecy fulfilled; but that is only because we are submerged. We look forward to events predicted and backward to events that have occurred; but God contains past and future in His own all-encompassing Being. To Him every event has already occurred, or perhaps it would be more accurate to say it is occurring. With Him there can never be a memory of things past nor an expectation of things to come, but only a knowledge of all things past and future as instantaneously present before His mind.

Everything that God is accords with all else that He is. Every thought He entertains is one with every other thought. His atitude toward sin and righteousness and life and death and human misery has not changed but remains exactly what it has been from the dark beginnings of precreation times before mankind had emerged into the stream of history.

The notion that the Old Testament differs radically from the New is erroneous. God wrote both and in them revealed certain spiritual laws which underlie all His creative and redemptive acts. These laws are one wherever they operate, in heaven or earth or hell. The Bible reveals God acting like Himself as He touches His creation; and an unchanging God is there seen acting according to moral and spiritual principles that can never change nor pass away.

In all this we must take into account the presence of sin, that evil mystery which for the time God permits to run amuck in the earth; or I should say that He is permitting it to run amuck in the universe— within certain sharply defined limits.

Sin has brought diversity, separation, dissimilarity, and has introduced divisions into a universe essentially one. Though we cannot hope now to understand this we must recognize it as a fact and withhold any final conclusion about it until the evidence is all in and we are by glorification morally and intellectually equipped to deal with it. Then it will be seen that God doeth all things well; now we are to believe without further proof. Faith reposes on the character of God and if we believe that God is perfect we must conclude that His ways are perfect also.

The concept of the unity of all things runs throughout the Sacred Scriptures. It is strongly emphasized in devotional theology and appears frequently in Christian hymnody. Such poets as Wordsworth made much of it. His long poem, "The Prelude," celebrates the organic unity of the world and shows every simple thing to be part of a created whole.

The work of Christ in redemption will achieve ultimately the expulsion of sin, the only divisive agent in the universe, and the unification of all things. "For it pleased the Father that in him should all fulness dwell; and, having made peace through the blood of his cross, by him to reconcile all things unto himself; by him, I say, whether they be things in earth, or things in heaven" (Col. 1:19, 20). The nearer the Christian soul comes to Christ in personal experience the more perfect becomes the internal unity even now.

The prophets and psalmists of the Old Testament wrestled as do we with the problem of evil in a divine universe, but their approach to God and nature was much more direct than ours. They did not interpose between God and His world that opaque web we moderns call the laws of nature. They could see God in a whirlwind and hear Him in a storm and they did not hesitate to say so. There was about their lives an immediate apprehension of the divine. They were not lonely amid impersonal laws as men are today. God was near to them, and everything in heaven and on earth assured them that this is God's world and that He rules over all.

I once heard a Methodist bishop say that when he was a very young minister he was called to the bedside of an elderly woman who had obviously but a few hours left for this world. The bishop admitted that he was badly frightened, but the old saint was completely relaxed and radiantly happy. He tried to commiserate with her and muttered something about how sorry he was that she had to die, but she wouldn't hear any such talk. "Why, God bless you, young man," she said cheerfully; "there's nothing to be scairt about. I'm just going to cross over Jordan in a few minutes, and my Father owns the land on both sides of the river."

She understood about the unity of all things.

Chapter 29

Nearness Is Likeness

ONE SERIOUS and often distressing problem for many Christians is their feeling that God is far from them, or that they are far from God, which is the same thing.

It is hard to rejoice in the Lord when we are suffering from this sense of remoteness. It is like trying to have a warm, bright summer without the sun. The chief trouble here is of course not intellectual and cannot be cured by intellectual means; yet truth must enter the mind before it can enter the heart, so let us reason together about this. In spiritual matters we think correctly only when we boldly rule out the concept of space. God is spirit, and spirit dwells not in space. Space has to do with matter and spirit is independent of it. By the concept of space we account for the relation of material bodies to each other.

We should never think of God as being spatially near or remote, for He is not here or there but carries here and there in His heart. Space is not infinite, as some have thought; only God is infinite and in His infinitude He swallows up all space. "Do not I fill heaven and earth? saith the Lord." He fills heaven and earth as the ocean fills the bucket that is submerged in it, and as the ocean surrounds the bucket so does God the universe He fills. "The heaven of heavens cannot contain thee." God is not contained: He contains.

As earthborn creatures we naturally tend to think by earthly analogies. "He that is of the earth is earthly, and speaketh of the earth." God created us living souls and gave us bodies through which we can experience the world around us and communicate with one another. When man fell through sin he began to think of himself as having a soul instead of being one. It makes a lot of difference whether a man believes that he is a body having a soul or a soul having a body.

The soul is inward and hidden, while the body is always present to the senses; consequently we tend to be body-conscious, and the concept of near and remote, which attaches to material things, seems quite natural to us. But it is valid only when it applies to moral creatures. When we try to apply it to God it no longer retains its validity.

Yet when we speak of men being "far" from God we speak truly. The Lord said of Israel, "Their heart is far from me," and there we have the definition of far and near in our relation to God. The words refer not to physical distance, but to likeness.

That God is equally near to all parts of His universe is plainly taught in the Scriptures (Psa. 139:1-18), yet some beings experience His nearness and others do not, depending upon their moral likeness to Him.

It is dissimilarity that creates the sense of remoteness between creatures and between men and God.

Two creatures may be so close physically that they touch, yet because of dissimilarity of nature be millions of miles apart. An angel and an ape might conceivably be in the same room, but the radical difference between their natures would make communion impossible. They would be "far" from each other in fact.

For the moral unlikeness between man and God the Bible has a word, alienation, and the Holy Spirit presents a frightful picture of this alienation as it works itself out in human character. Fallen human nature is precisely opposite to the nature of God as revealed in Jesus Christ. Because there is no moral likeness there is no communion, hence the sense of physical distance, the feeling that God is far away in space. This erroneous notion discourages prayer and prevents many a sinner from believing unto life.

Paul encouraged the Athenians by reminding them that God was not far from any one of them, that it was He in whom they lived and moved and had their being. Yet men think of Him as farther away than the farthest star. The truth is that He is nearer to us than we are to ourselves.

But how can the conscious sinner bridge the mighty gulf that separates him from God in living experience? The answer is that he cannot, but the glory of the Christian message is that Christ did. Through the blood of His cross He made peace that He might reconcile all things unto Himself. "And you, that were

121

sometime alienated and enemies in your mind by wicked works, yet now hath he reconciled in the body of his flesh through death, to present you holy and unblameable and unreproveable in his sight" (Col. 1:21, 22).

The new birth makes us partakers of the divine nature. There the work of undoing the dissimilarity between us and God begins. From there it progresses by the sanctifying operation of the Holy Spirit till God is satisfied.

That is the theology of it, but as I said, even the regenerated soul may sometimes suffer from the feeling that God is far from Him. What then should he do?

First, the trouble may be no more than a temporary break in God-conscious communion due to any one of half a hundred causes. The cure is faith. Trust God in the dark till the light returns.

Second, should the sense of remoteness persist in spite of prayer and what you believe is faith, look to your inner life for evidences of wrong attitudes, evil thoughts or dispositional flaws. These are unlike God and create a psychological gulf between you and Him. Put away the evil from you, believe, and the sense of nearness will be restored. God was never away in the first place.

Chapter 30

Work and Worship

To UNDERSTAND the relative importance of work and worship it is necessary to know the answer to the familiar question, "What is the chief end of man?" The answer given in the catechism, "To glorify God and to enjoy Him forever," can scarcely be improved upon, though of course it is an outline only and needs to be enlarged somewhat if it is to be a full and satisfying answer.

The primary purpose of God in creation was to prepare moral beings spiritually and intellectually capable of worshiping Him. This has been so widely accepted by theologians and Bible expositors through the centuries that I shall make no attempt to prove it here. It is fully taught in the Scriptures and demonstrated abundantly in the lives of the saints. We may safely receive it as axiomatic and go on from there.

Once God existed in ineffable perfection of beauty with only the Persons of the Triune God to know and love each other.

"When heaven and earth were yet unmade,
When time was yet unknown,

> *Thou in Thy bliss and majesty*
> *Didst live and love alone."*

Then God brought into being all things "that are in heaven, and that are in earth, visible and invisible, whether they be thrones, or dominions, or principalities, or powers: all things were created by him, and for him."

> *"How wonderful creation is.*
> *The work that Thou didst bless,*
> *And, oh! what then must Thou be like,*
> *Eternal Loveliness!"*

God is the essence of all beauty, the fountain of all spiritual sweetness that can be known or desired by moral beings. He can and does love Himself with an unutterably holy love which we fallen creatures can gaze upon only with veiled faces and about which we dare speak only with hushed reverence and with humble admission of all but total ignorance.

By that moral disaster known in theology as the fall of man an entire order of beings was wrenched violently loose from its proper place in the creational scheme and quite literally turned upside down. Human beings who had been specifically created to admire and adore the Deity turned away from Him and began to pour out their love first upon themselves and then upon whatever cheap and tawdry objects their lusts and passions found. The first chapter of Romans describes the journey of the human heart downward from the knowledge of God to the basest idolatry and fleshly sins. History is little more than the story of man's sin, and the daily newspaper a running commentary on it.

The work of Christ in redemption, for all its mystery, has a simple and understandable end: it is to restore men to the position from which they fell and bring them around again to be admirers and lovers of the Triune God. God saves men to make them worshipers.

This great central fact has been largely forgotten today, not by the liberals and the cults only, but by evangelical Christians as well. By direct teaching, by story, by example, by psychological pressure we force our new converts to "go to work for the Lord." Ignoring the fact that God has redeemed them to make worshipers out of them, we thrust them out into "service," quite as if the Lord were recruiting laborers for a project instead of seeking to restore moral beings to a condition where they can glorify God and enjoy Him forever.

This is not to say that there is not work to be done; most certainly there is, and God in His condescending love works in and through His redeemed children. Our Lord commands us to pray the Lord of the harvest that He will send forth laborers into His harvest field. What we are overlooking is that no one can be a worker who is not first a worshiper. Labor that does not spring out of worship is futile and can only be wood, hay and stubble in the day that shall try every man's works.

It may be set down as an axiom that if we do not worship we cannot work acceptably. The Holy Spirit can work through a worshiping heart and through no other kind. We may go through the motions and delude ourselves by our religious activity, but we are setting ourselves up for a shocking disillusionment some day.

Without doubt the emphasis in Christian teaching today should be on worship. There is little danger that we shall become merely worshipers and neglect the practical implications of the gospel. No one can long worship God in spirit and in truth before the obligation to holy service becomes too strong to resist. Fellowship with God leads straight to obedience and good works. That is the divine order and it can never be reversed.

Chapter 31

The Powers
That Shape Us

FORTUNATELY FOR ALL of us, human nature is not fixed but plastic. Every human being is in a state of becoming, of passing from what he was to what he is to be. And this is as true of the Christian as of every other person.

The new birth does not produce the finished product. The new thing that is born of God is as far from completeness as the new baby born an hour ago. That new human being, the moment he is born, is placed in the hands of powerful molding forces that go far to determine whether he shall be an upright citizen or a criminal. The one hope for him is that he can later choose which forces shall shape him, and by the exercise of his own power of choice he can place himself in the right hands. In that sense he shapes himself and is responsible at last for the outcome.

It is not otherwise with the Christian. He can fashion himself by placing himself in the hands first of the supreme Artist, God, and then by subjecting himself to such holy influences and such formative powers as shall make him into a man of God. Or he may foolishly trust himself to unworthy hands and become at last a misshapen and inartistic vessel, of little use to mankind and a poor example of the skill of the heavenly Potter.

To any who might object that we cannot fashion ourselves, that God alone can fashion us, we offer this explanation: A young man decides he wants the benefits of a healthy tan. Now, does he tan himself or does the sun tan him? Of course the answer is that he tans himself by exposing himself to the sun. He has but to bring himself into contact with the sun's rays and the sun will take care of the rest.

So we fashion ourselves by exposing our lives to the molding influences, good or bad, that lie around us. Let us pull this thought down from the theoretical to the practical and identify some of the powers that shape us.

FRIENDS. We are all influenced powerfully by our companions. Even the strongest characters are shaped by the company they keep. They may flatter themselves that they, with their dominant personalities, are shaping others and are uninfluenced by the lives of their friends; but we cannot escape the power of friendships.

LITERATURE. What we read with enjoyment does much to decide what we shall be finally. To lend the mind to the spell of a book is to become clay in the potter's hand. In our Protestant system no one can decide what we shall read, but what we read will shape us for good or evil.

128

MUSIC. There is about music a subtle charm that no normal person can resist. It works to condition the mind and prepare it for the reception of ideas, moral and immoral, which in turn prepare the will to act either in righteousness or in sin. The notion that music and song are merely for amusement and that their effects can be laughed off is a deadly error. Actually they exercise a powerful creative influence over the plastic human soul. And their permanent effects will be apparent in our growth in grace or in evil.

PLEASURES. The human constitution is so constructed that it requires a certain amount of pleasure; it is built for it as a harp is built for music, and remains incomplete and unfulfilled without it. Sin lies not in receiving pleasure but in deriving it from wrong objects. A mother tending her baby in a glow of delight or smiling in death when she hears that her late-born is normal and will live presents a tender picture of unselfish pleasure. A man at the card table fascinated by the thrills and perils of gambling is an example of degraded and demoralizing pleasure. The Christian should look well to his pleasures for they will ennoble or debase him, and this by a secret law of the soul from which there is no escape.

AMBITIONS. The great saints of the world have all been ambitious. They were driven forward by an inward urge that finally became too much for them. Paul stated his ambition as being a desire to know Christ and to enter into the fullest meaning of His death and resurrection, and toward this goal he pressed with everything that lay in him. By this

129

ambition he was propelled upward to the very peak of spiritual perfection. Carnal and selfish ambitions, however, have just the opposite effect. Each one should watch his ambitions, for they will shape him as an artist shapes the yielding clay.

THOUGHTS. We Christians need to take into account the tremendous power that lies in plain, ordinary thinking. We have allowed ourselves to be cheated out of a precious treasure by the irresponsible babblings of weird occultists and quack religionists who make too much of the human mind or who misunderstand it altogether. From them we have turned away, and have turned so far that we forget that it is still true that a man will finally be what his active thoughts make him. It is hardly too much to say that no Christian ever fell into sin who did not first allow himself to brood over it with increasing desire. And every godly soul knows how much spiritual meditations have meant to the total success of his inward life. "As (a man) thinketh in his heart, so is he."

There are of course many others, but these are among the major forces that shape our lives. To sum up, the wise Christian will take advantage of every proper means of grace and every ennobling and purifying influence that God in His providence places in his way. Conversely, he will avoid every degrading influence and flee from those forces that make for evil. He has but to coöperate with God in embracing the good. God himself will do the rest.

Chapter 32

Why We Are Lukewarm About Christ's Return

SHORTLY AFTER the close of the first World War, I heard a great Southern preacher say that he feared the intense interest in prophecy current at that time would result in a dying out of the blessed hope when events had proved the excited interpreters wrong.

The man was a prophet, or at least a remarkably shrewd student of human nature, for exactly what he predicted has come to pass. The hope of Christ's coming is today all but dead among evangelicals.

I do not mean that Bible Christians have given up the doctrine of the second advent. By no means. There has been, as every informed person knows, an adjustment among some of the lesser tenets of our prophetic credo, but the vast majority of evangelicals continue to hold to the belief that Jesus Christ will sometime actually come back to the earth in person. The ultimate triumph of Christ is accepted as one of the unshakable doctrines of Holy Scripture.

It is true that in some quarters the prophecies of the Bible are occasionally expounded. This is especially so among Hebrew Christians who, for reasons well understood, seem to feel closer to the prophets of the Old Testament than do Gentile believers. Their love for their own people naturally leads them to grasp at every hope of the conversion and ultimate restoration of Israel. To many of them the return of Christ represents a quick and happy solution of the "Jewish problem." The long centuries of wandering will end when He comes and God will at that time "restore again the kingdom to Israel." We dare not allow our deep love for our Hebrew Christian brethren to blind us to the obvious political implications of this aspect of their Messianic hope. We do not blame them for this. We merely call attention to it.

Yet the return of Christ as a blessed hope is, as I have said, all but dead among us. The truth touching the second advent, where it is presented today, is for the most part either academic or political. The joyful personal element is altogether missing. Where are they who

"Yearn for the sign, O Christ, of thy fulfilling,
Faint for the flaming of Thine advent feet"?

The longing to see Christ that burned in the breasts of those first Christians seems to have burned itself out. All we have left are the ashes. It is precisely the "yearning" and the "fainting" for the return of Christ that has distinguished the personal hope from the theological one. Mere acquaintance with correct doctrine is a poor substitute for Christ and familiarity with New Testament eschatology will never take the place of a love-inflamed desire to look on His face.

132

If the tender yearning is gone from the advent hope today there must be a reason for it; and I think I know what it is, or what they are, for there are a number of them. One is simply that popular fundamentalist theology has emphasized the utility of the cross rather than the beauty of the One who died on it. The saved man's relation to Christ has been made contractual instead of personal. The "work" of Christ has been stressed until it has eclipsed the person of Christ. Substitution has been allowed to supersede identification. What He did for me seems to be more important than what He is to me. Redemption is seen as an across-the-counter transaction which we "accept," and the whole thing lacks emotional content. We must love someone very much to stay awake and long for his coming, and that may explain the absence of power in the advent hope even among those who still believe in it.

Another reason for the absence of real yearning for Christ's return is that Christians are so comfortable in this world that they have little desire to leave it. For those leaders who set the pace of religion and determine its content and quality, Christianity has become of late remarkably lucrative. The streets of gold do not have too great an appeal for those who find it so easy to pile up gold and silver in the service of the Lord here on earth. We all want to reserve the hope of heaven as a kind of insurance against the day of death, but as long as we are healthy and comfortable, why change a familiar good for something about which we actually know very little? So reasons the

133

carnal mind, and so subtly that we are scarcely aware of it.

Again, in these times religion has become jolly good fun right here in this present world, and what's the hurry about heaven anyway? Christianity, contrary to what some had thought, is another and higher form of entertainment. Christ has done all the suffering. He has shed all the tears and carried all the crosses; we have but to enjoy the benefits of His heartbreak in the form of religious pleasures modeled after the world but carried on in the name of Jesus. So say the same people who claim to believe in Christ's second coming.

History reveals that times of suffering for the Church have also been times of looking upward. Tribulation has always sobered God's people and encouraged them to look for and yearn after the return of their Lord. Our present preoccupation with this world may be a warning of bitter days to come. God will wean us from the earth some way—the easy way if possible, the hard way if necessary. It is up to us.

Chapter 33

Our Hope of Future Blessedness

GOD BEING A GOD of infinite goodness must by the necessity of His nature will for each of His creatures the fullest measure of happiness consistent with its capacities and with the happiness of all other creatures.

Furthermore, being omniscient and omnipotent, God has the wisdom and power to achieve whatever He wills. The redemption which He wrought for us through the incarnation, death and resurrection of His only-begotten Son guarantees eternal blessedness to all who through faith become beneficiaries of that redemption.

This the Church teaches her children to believe, and her teaching is more than hopeful thinking. It is founded upon the fullest and plainest revelations of the Old and New Testaments. That it accords with the most sacred yearnings of the human heart does not in any manner weaken it, but serves rather to confirm the truth of it, since the One who made the heart might be expected also to make provision for the fulfillment of its deepest longings.

While Christians believe this in a general way it is still difficult for them to visualize life as it will be in heaven, and it is especially hard for them to picture themselves as inheriting such bliss as the Scriptures describe. The reason for this is not hard to discover. The most godly Christian is the one who knows himself best, and no one who knows himself will believe that he deserves anything better than hell.

The man who knows himself least is likely to have a cheerful if groundless confidence in his own moral worth. Such a man has less trouble believing that he will inherit an eternity of bliss because his concepts are only quasi-Christian, being influenced strongly by chimney-corner scripture and old wives' tales. He thinks of heaven as being very much like California without the heat and the smog, and himself as inhabiting a splendiferous palace with all modern conveniences, and wearing a heavily bejeweled crown. Throw in a few angels and you have the vulgar picture of the future life held by the devotees of popular Christianity.

This is the heaven that appears in the saccharin ballads of the guitar-twanging rockabilly gospellers that clutter up the religious scene today. That the whole thing is completely unrealistic and contrary to the laws of the moral universe seems to make no difference to anyone. As a pastor I have laid to rest the mortal remains of many a man whose future could not but be mighty uncertain, but who before the funeral was over nevertheless managed to get title to a mansion just over the hilltop. I have steadfastly refused to utter any word that would add to the deception, but the emotional wattage of the singing was so high that the mourners went away vaguely believing that in spite of all they knew about the deceased everything would be all right some bright morning.

No one who has felt the weight of his own sin or heard from Calvary the Saviour's mournful cry, "My God, my God, why hast thou forsaken me?" can ever allow his soul to rest on the feeble hope popular religion affords. He will—indeed he must—insist upon forgiveness and cleansing and the protection the vicarious death of Christ provides.

"God has made him who knew no sin to be sin for us, that we might be made the righteousness of God in him." So wrote Paul, and Luther's great outburst of faith shows what this can mean in a human soul. "O Lord," cried Luther, "Thou art my righteousness, I am Thy sin."

Any valid hope of a state of blessedness beyond the incident of death must lie in the goodness of God and the work of atonement accomplished for us by Jesus Christ on the cross. The deep, deep love of God is the fountain out of which flows our future beatitude, and the grace of God in Christ is the channel by which it reaches us. The cross of Christ creates a moral situation where every attribute of God is on the side of the returning sinner. Even justice is on our side, for it is written, "If we confess our sins, he is

137

faithful and just to forgive us our sins, and to cleanse us from all unrighteousness."

The true Christian may safely look forward to a future state that is as happy as perfect love wills it to be. Since love cannot desire for its object anything less than the fullest possible measure of enjoyment for the longest possible time, it is virtually beyond our power to conceive of a future as consistently delightful as that which Christ is preparing for us. And who is to say what is possible with God?

Chapter 34

Joy Will Come
in Its Own Time

WE CAN KNOW our present properly only as we know our past, and in that past there occurred something disgraceful and tragic, namely, the loss of our moral character and rebellion against our Creator. That we also lost our happiness is of secondary importance, since it is but a result of our alienation from God and not a part of that alienation.

The primary work of Christ in redemption is to justify, sanctify and ultimately to glorify a company of persons salvaged from the ruin of the human race.

For the convenience of any who may not be familiar with the words used here I would explain that justify means to declare righteous before God, sanctify means to make holy, and glorify means in effect to remake the entire personality after the image of Christ. This will fit us to dwell eternally in that heaven about which the Bible speaks and which is both a state of being and a location. In that heaven the ransomed will experience unclouded communion with the Triune God; and that will itself assure unalloyed blessedness.

I have just now used the word "ruin" and associated it with the human race. This is not a figure of speech nor is it an extravagant or irresponsible use of a word. The race lies in ruin, spiritually, morally and physically. History and the daily newspaper testify to our moral ruin. The long parade of gods, both virtuous and obscene, and a thousand varieties of vain and meaningless religious practices declare our spiritual degeneration, while disease, old age and death testify sadly to the completeness of our physical decay.

We inhabit a world suspended halfway between heaven and hell, alienated from one and not yet abandoned to the other. By nature we are unholy and by practice unrighteous. That we are also unhappy, I repeat, is of small consequence. Our first and imperative duty is to escape the corruption which is in the world as Lot escaped the moral ruin of Sodom. It is of overwhelming importance to us that we should seek the favor of God while it is possible to find it and that we should bring ourselves under the plenary authority of Jesus Christ in complete and voluntary obedience. To do this is to invite trouble from a hostile world and to incur such unhappiness as may naturally follow. Add to this the temptations of the devil and a lifelong struggle with the flesh and it will be obvious that we will need to defer most of our enjoyments to a more appropriate time.

Against this background of fact our childish desire to be happy is seen to be a morally ugly thing, wholly foreign to the Spirit of the Man of Sorrows and contrary to the teaching and practice of His apostles.

Any appeal to the public in the name of Christ that rises no higher than an invitation to tranquillity must be recognized as mere humanism with a few words of Jesus thrown in to make it appear Christian. But only that is truly Christian which accords with the spirit and teachings of Christ. Everything else is unChristian or anti-Christian, no matter whence it emanates.

Strange, is it not, that we dare without shame to alter, to modulate the words of Christ while speaking for Christ to the very ones for whom He died?

Christ calls men to carry a cross; we call them to have fun in His name. He calls them to forsake the world; we assure them that if they but accept Jesus the world is their oyster. He calls them to suffer; we call them to enjoy all the bourgeois comforts modern civilization affords. He calls them to self-abnegation and death; we call them to spread themselves like green bay trees or perchance even to become stars in a pitiful fifth-rate religious zodiac. He calls them to holiness; we call them to a cheap and tawdry happiness that would have been rejected with scorn by the least of the Stoic philosophers.

In a world like this, with conditions being what they are, what should a serious-minded Christian do? The answer is easy to give but hard to follow.

First, accept the truth concerning yourself. You do not go to a doctor to seek consolation but to find out what is wrong and what to do about it. Seek the kingdom of God and His righteousness. Seek through Jesus Christ a right relation to God and then insist upon maintaining a right relationship to your fellow man. Set about reverently to amend your doings. Magnify God, mortify the flesh, simplify your life. Take up your cross and learn of Jesus Christ to die to this world that He may raise you up in due time.

If you will do these things in faith and love, you will know peace, but it will be the peace of God that passes all understanding. You will know joy, but it will be the joy of resurrection, not the irresponsible happiness of men who insist on carnal enjoyments. You will know the comfort of the indwelling Spirit which will often spring up like a well of water in the desert, not because you have sought it but have sought rather to do the will of God at any price.

We can afford to suffer now; we'll have a long eternity to enjoy ourselves. And our enjoyment will be valid and pure, for it will come in the right way at the right time.